MW01293201

*Presented To:*

_____

*From:*

_____

*Date:*

_____

# I AM PROPHECY
## Prophetic Preliminaries Vol. 1

# I AM PROPHECY
## Prophetic Preliminaries Vol. 1
## Orin Perry

Orin Perry Ministries Inc.
www.orinperry.com
P.O Box 517
Roanoke Rapids N.C. 27870

ISBN: 978-1-365-82031-1

LIFE More Publishing, Richmond, VA

# DEDICATION

I dedicate this book to God and the Legacy of Claude and Lola Perry.

Mrs. Masa Kinsey-Shipp (Mrs. Shipp) for your heartfelt guidance as my first administrator and mentor for my success.

# ACKNOWLEDGEMENTS

All praise, honor, and glory goes to God (Christ Jesus) who is not first in my life but is the essence of my life. Without His grace, wisdom, and favor I could not function or complete my divine fulfilling purpose in the earth realm. I thank God for my church the House of Mandate Inc. of Roanoke Rapids, N.C, for their prayers, time, and support. To my awesome administrative staff, for your tirelessly volunteering and dedication.

To my spiritual father the honorable Bishop Glen. A. Staples who graced me with the favor of man as John the Baptist did Christ in the book of Mark (the one that paved the way for my success). Your teachings have given me the strength to walk in excellence and grace even under pressure. The precept of endurance has been one of the greatest principles being applied yet. Knowing how to suffer with 'class', I do know now suffering is the platform for your NEXT (1 Peter 5:10)!

Beyond words, expressions, oxymorons, and punctuation, I pause and honor my mom (Prophet Mary Perry-Howell). I could not do this without you, how your wisdom, knowledge, and correction pushes me. THIS BOOK LITERALLY IS WISDOM AND KNOWLEDGE THAT YOU HAVE DOWNLOADED INTO ME FROM LATE NIGHT CONVERSATIONS AND THAT NURTURING PUSH TO STUDY GOD'S WORD FOR MYSELF. Who would have thought your wisdom would be echoed and read for centuries to come. As I wrote this book, I heard your voice saying, "just furnish GOD a life". I thank you and I LOVE YOU.

Eric, Brandon, Meoshia, Tobias, all my nephews and nieces, and MICAI --- I love you all!! CAN ANY GOOD THING COME OUT OF US?

# ENDORSEMENTS

*"I Am Prophecy is one of the most comprehensive, well-written, insightful teachings for this millennial generation. The hidden core mysteries of the prophetic, which includes character, integrity, intact-fullness, and God's grace, are all unraveled. With the recalcitrant operations of 'Witchcraft in the Pews', it's going to take true prophetic comprehension and divine power with God to eradicate the works of Satan. The revelation that God has downloaded through Prophet Orin Perry in this book will dismantle satanic strongholds and give insight to the hidden places of the prophetic. Are you ready to accept that you are Prophecy?"*

**Bishop George G. Bloomer**
**Author, National Televangelist, International Lecturer**
**Durham, North Carolina**

*"Prophet Perry is an anointed voice to the Body of Christ with an accurate prophetic gift. His insight shared in this book will enlighten and encourage the kingdom of God at large."*

**Bishop Eric McDaniel**
**Pastor, Lecturer, National Recording Artist**
**Bronx, New York | Raleigh, North Carolina**

*"This book is a deep dive into the prophetic. A powerful discussion of its meaning, its intended use and the great call of God to be chosen as his Prophet! Thank you Prophet Perry for articulating such a thoughtful book and helping all those ready to realize I Am Prophecy!"*

**Antar Muhammad**
**Motivational Lecturer | Author**
**Antar Muhammad Ministries Inc.**
**Dallas, Texas**

# I AM PRINCIPLES

# FOREWORD
Bishop Glen A. Staples, Th.D.

In him we were also chosen, having been
predestined according to the plan of him who works out
everything in conformity with the purpose of his will,
**Ephesians 1:11 (New International Version)**

Prophecy is simply a message of divine truth that reveals the will of God. Every one of us has a God ordained prophecy that has to be fulfilled – I am a witness, it will come to past. Some of us spend our entire lives living out the prophetic assignment that has been placed over our individual lives. The key to fulfilling your prophecy is to solely understand that *YOU* are prophecy… *I Am Prophecy*… we are all prophecy… before there was time, God spoke over your life a prophecy that only you could fulfill.

The author of this phenomenal book is someone who I have witnessed firsthand mature and become wise beyond his years through the preaching and teaching of the Word of God. A true and authentic vessel willing to be used by God, *Prophet Orin Perry*, is one of God's prophets.

There is a need for authentic prophetic voices in the Earth now more than ever. With the uncertainty of leadership around the world, people are yearning for a sound of hope, love and compassion. These are distinct traits that reside within *Prophet Perry's* character and that is why I am honored to pin this foreword for this wonderful literary and anointed manuscript, "*I Am Prophecy*."

Understanding what it means to be prophecy and how to operate under a prophecy, *Prophet Perry* takes you on an intellectual prophetic journey page by page through "*I Am Prophecy*." The narrative on these pages will serve as a manual for any person that is called to be a prophetic voice in the Earth yet will also provide clarity to those individuals who understand that their life is a prophecy.

*Prophet Perry* illustrates the importance of functioning in the prophetic but also how to comprehend the prophetic. This teaching is only a glimpse of the anointing that rests on the life of this prophetic gift that I have been able to witness. I am extremely proud of him and I know this is only the beginning for what is to come in his life. I invite you to take this journey with him as you explore the chapters of this book, I encourage you to be open to receive everything that God has for you.

It brings me great joy to introduce to the Body of Christ this prophetic gift, my son in the gospel, ***Prophet Orin Perry***.

Bishop Glen A. Staples

# INTRODUCTION
# THE DIAGNOSTIC OF PROPHETIC
# PRELIMINARIES

Prophetic Preliminaries provides an appurtenant of phrases, statements, and slogans for the prophetic realm of the Christian ministry. Each phrase is scripturally defined with in depth revelatory insight. The term *preliminary* is defined as the introductory or initial stage of an entity. This book serves as a guide and manual for beginning prophetic officiants/vessels on how to function in the prophetic ministry that aligns with heaven and earth. From this book, you will not only get answers for questions concerning the prophetic, but practical insight to assist with the prophetic realm. This book provides you with mandates that must be aligned in practicality to be effective in modern day ministry for the prophetic ministry.

Prophetic Preliminaries enlightens the reader by strategically expounding on laws, supernatural legislations, and divine policies of the supernatural that must be kept in order to function in God's divine grace in the prophetic ministry. As the earth realm has laws that assist the development and function of the earth so does the prophetic realm. You are in for an extraordinary enlightenment in the supernatural by taken the time to apprehend the wisdom of the prophetic DNA of your spirit man.

Artlessly, not everything can be written or expounded upon in a book, nor should it even be attempted. Therefore, Prophetic Preliminaries is not prepped as a full course meal, but to give you a capsule of information that will jumpstart your journey in your spiritual maturation in the prophetic. Because of this, you should be careful in your usage of this book in not making this your guide but a supplement to the Bible the living word (logos) of God. It is meant for prophetic purposes only, and therefore, readers should beware of reading these Prophetic Preliminaries without solemnly committing to the protocol of the prophetic and supernatural realm with foundational biblical truths.

People from every walk of life can reap the benefits of this book, serving as a tool that can bring structure to the understanding of the supernatural realm and the prophetic ministry God Himself has graced the church with.

# THE EMINENCE OF PROPHETIC PRELIMINARIES

The vitalness of Prophetic Preliminaries is equivalent to the success of any industry in gathering organized wisdom. The best way in accomplishing success in any profession is the endeavor to comprehend protocols, policies, and regulations. Uniformed discipline tactics and learning the unlearned of any enterprise by collecting, organizing, and accurately defining responses and procedures enhances the advancement of anyone.

*In layman terms understanding the do's and don'ts of any operation quickly promotes or demotes.*

For prophetic officiants/vessels to receive the honor and respect in their vocation, there must be an aggregation of divine wisdom, knowledge, and comprehension. With these attributes, accurate prophetic delivery in any vocation of the prophetic is inevitable. A prophetic officiant/vessel will function in an expeditious manner in seeing stability, legitimization, and authoritative actions in the supernatural realm. For this very reason, prophetic officiants/vessels need a cohesive means of understanding the legislations of the heavens. That need declares the clarion call for the revealing of heavens legislations, which is found within this book. Being that God does nothing within the earth realm without the revealing unto the His prophet's and prophetic officiants/vessels (Amos 3:7 KJV), this constitutes that all prophetic officiants/vessels must understand the decrees of heaven and how to rightly divide them. Authentic prophets and prophetic officiants/vessels acknowledge that there are unique operations within the prophetic realm. Each operation is distinct, vastly defined, and divinely articulated but all operations must submit to the legislations, policies, and rules of heaven to be distinguishably called the Lord's bidding. Often modern day prophets and prophetic officiants/vessels are inadequately used and administered in the compass of amiss

(James 4:3 KJV) or defiled by carnal administration or demonic domain, when there is a break or breach of supernatural legislation. For example, prophets and prophetic officiants/vessels give universal prophecy or give words of knowledge and wisdom. When not comprehending the divine legislation of Mark 6:4 KVJ, "A prophet is not without honor in his own country", the prophet or prophetic officiants/vessels must detach from his/her kinsmen in order to effectively function in the call of the prophetic. Another factor of this divine legislation is when honor is not found amongst those who bleed the same DNA of a prophet or prophetic officiant/vessel but as God told Abraham get thee out from your kinsmen (Gen. 12:1 KJV) then and only then can you deliver what you are detached from. In addition, Prophetic Preliminaries gives credence to the many why's prophets and prophetic officiants/vessels have in the dismantling of their goals and plans, being that God Himself governs the steps of the prophetic voice.

Along with the many legislations of heaven, are the legislations of the earth, and the ordinances of the institute of the church. Comprehending how to operate in the earth and in the many personality built ministries is essential. Promptly grasping the ordinances of the church to exhaust the rationalization and excuses of rejection by knowing that a prophetic is subject to a prophet (1 Cor. 14:32 KJV). The need of the unveiling of Prophetic Preliminaries is needed more than ever as oxygen is to the humanity so stands order to the prophetic grace of heaven.

# PROPHETIC LESSONS OF PROTOCOL

The Bible supports and gives assurance to methods of prophetic preparation. It presents accounts of ministerial mishandling, prophetic dishonor, and a diverse disarray of a chaotic infrastructure of corruption in the prophetic realm. From Balaam the Prophet, Joram and Jambres, King Herod, Ham, and Achan the accursed one; and a vast majority of others are not only biblical examples of divine breeches in the supernatural realm but also lessons of protocol in the prophetic. Therefore the ability to rightly divide the words and declarations of the Lord gives for the productive application to ready the earth for the coming of the Lord is more vital than any other function. This function is given to the office and graces of the prophetic.

Prophetic Preliminaries equips unto the place that the prophetic officiant/vessel can skillfully be used in uniting the church, and competently bring the word of the Lord to pass on the earth. Have you ever wondered why every biblically known prophet served with a mantle in hand, there is a prophetic lesson locked in that principle. Examine, for instance, the Lord's Prophet Elijah who passed the mantle of the prophet to his servant and successor Elisha (2 Kings 2: 12-13 KJV). Since Elisha had the assignment to combat the residue and forces of Ahab and Jezebel, God used the mantle of Elisha's predecessor Elijah. The mantle was just not a transference of power but prophetic protocol. God used the mantle as a phenomenon to show forth the divine legislation of prophetic protocol. When the voice of a preliminary prophet is submitted, silenced, and secured then and only then they can function in the DNA of the originating prophet. Being that there is no original anointing or an anointing that is generated or granted by oneself, every prophet must find themselves under the tutelage of another acting prophet. A submitted prophet must be a *disengaged* prophet to develop into an *engaged* prophet before maturation is granted or seen. The Prophet Elisha was found in 1 Kings 19:19-21 disengaged, by the engaged Prophet Elijah. Elisha was then *submitted*, *silenced*, and *secured* by the Prophet Elijah, this act within the guidelines of this Prophetic Preliminary guaranteed ministerial covenant and affirmation.

To validate the prophetic ministry of a vessel, it's imperative that divine legislations and laws are kept in order to function in kingdom alignment with heaven. Otherwise, the breech of divine legislations makes it impossible to develop a holistic stance on earth and in heaven. The secrets of God will remain secrets and the voice of heaven will be silenced. With this tool Prophetic Preliminaries, every hinderance that causes divine malfunctions in the prophetic realm will be denounced and illuminated, being that these tools highlight the how and the why of the prophetic ministry.

# I AM PROPHECY
# PRINCIPLE ONE:
# CARNAL PROPHECIES

**"PROFICIENT PROPHECY IS MORE VITAL THAN THE ARTICULATION OF WORDS. ADDING WORDS WITHOUT DIVINE CONSENT WILL POLLUTE PROPHECY."**

*"You shall not add to the word that I command you, nor take from it, that you may keep the commandments of the Lord you God that I command you." Deuteronomy 4:2 KJV*

Every prophetic word must be channeled through the trichotomy of a man, before released in the earth realm. The challenge comes when the prophetic word given to the spirit of man has to channel through the soul of the man, and then be released through the physicality of man or a prophetic vessel. Being that God saved our spirits, and has to transform our minds according to Rom. 12:1-3 KJV, the pollution of the soul can become fragmented on the word from God. The risk of old mindsets with a renewed spirit is the danger of carnal decisions with a divine destiny. As we know the word of God states, "there is no good thing in the flesh" (Rom. 7:12 KJV), abortion is inevitable with a carnal act with a divine mandate. Assumptions, premeditated conclusions, conjectures, or opinions added to the word of God are as venom to the human body. Opinions cause more harm than help, damage than development, and deception than conception. Words frame worlds (Heb. 11:3 KJV), therefore the wrong phrasing can frame a world of life (prosperity, health, and blessings) or a world of death (lack, chaos, and voidness). A perverted prophecy can and will strip anyone of their future inheritance.

The danger of the 21st century is that many seek intelligence, which can ultimately cancel out obedience. Being that God voiced he takes the ignorant things to profound the wise

(1 Cor. 1:27 KJV). A hypothesis (educated guess) will never bring manifestation only the proficient and precise word from God can. Every word from God must be echoed exactly as the Word of God; via divine precision God will prompt manifestation. Deliverance from opinions is pivotal in the realm of the prophetic. Do not add or subtract from the Word of God, it is complete, whole, and fulfilled without humanistic support, verbiage, and intelligence.

## Heresy

When a prophetic vessel operates from a carnal realm he/she is subject to releasing heresy and carnal prophesies as Balaam the prophet did in the book of Numbers (Num. 22 1-35 KJV). Speaking from the emotions, will, and intellect prohibit true divine intervention. Carnal Prophecies always appease the flesh and the host of the word, but never perform or ignite the will of God in the receptors life. 2 Tim. 4:3(KJV) is the verse of enlightenment that tells us the effects of carnal prophecies. *"For the time will come when they will not endure sound doctrine; but after their own lusts shall they heap to themselves teachers, having itching ears; And they shall turn away their ears from the truth, and shall be turned unto fables."*

***Heresy is "an opinion, doctrine, or practice contrary to the truth or to generally accepted beliefs or standards"[1] The Apostle Paul warned us about false prophets and teachers. These are ones who distort the truth for personal motive or gain. Remember that true prophecy brings order and completion, but false prophecy brings division and destruction.***

---

[1] Heresy, Merriam-Webster Online Dictionary copyright © 2014 by Merriam-Webster, Incorporated.http://www.merriam-webster.com/dictionary/heresy. (accessed February 20, 2014)

*"Who has spoken and it came to pass, unless the Lord has command it?" Lamentations 3:37 ESV*

*"Everything that I command you, you shall be careful to do. You shall not add to it or take from it." Deuteronomy 12:32 ESV*

*"I warn everyone who hears the words of the prophecy of this book: If anyone adds to them, God will add to him the plagues described in this book." Revelation 22:18 ESV*

# I AM PROPHECY
# PRINCIPLE TWO:
# IMMACULATE OR CONTAMINATE

> **"THE ALTER-EGO OF THE PROPHETIC IS PERVERSION. SERVING AS THE TWIN OF THE PROPHETIC, PERVERSION IS ANYTHING THAT WITHDRAWS PURITY OR DISTORTS RIGHTEOUSNESS."**

*"For prophecy never came by the will of man, but HOLY men of God spoke as they were moved by the Holy Spirit." 2 Peter 1:21 KJV*

The vice to pure prophetic virtue is perversion, becoming defiled, polluted, contaminated, and/or corrupt. Perversion in short term is called SIN. Sin is very contagious; in so that the 3 dimensions of sin are always opened for us to travel through. Thought, Action, and Voice are all vacuums to sin which defiles a vessel. Sin is identical to dust no matter what we do we will collect it; no matter how much we clean, we must continue to cleanse and clean. Many do not understand the vitalness of cleanness.

## Internal Cleanness

I have a brief allegorical memory for you, which can bring exceptional clarification to this prophetic principle. As a young man growing up I would have to do chores and one of my many chores was washing dishes. My mother had a fine china dinnerware set that she wanted cleaned very well. Many times, I would clean with perfection, but this particular day I was washing from a near comatose disposition and as you figured, I ended up washing a dirty cup. As you know the next time the cup was used the particles from the previous usage was swimming in the beverage in the cup. My mother went to use the cup only to find that the beverage she poured had particles in it from the cups previous user and usage. It was not the pourers fault, it was not the beverage fault, it was not even the previous user's fault, it was the washer's fault. Reason being it was not cleaned for the next use. The necessity of being clean is more essential than being used. Psalm 24:3-4 (KJV) asks the million-dollar question and gives the billion-dollar answer. "Who can ascend into the holy hill of the Lord? Or who shall stand in his holy place? He that hath clean hands, and a pure heart; who hath not lifted up his soul (mind) into vanity, nor sworn deceitfully."

Growing up in strict apostolic tenets we were taught that if you furnish God a life, he will do the rest. Present God a HOLY life and he will use you to usher in a HOLY people. The way to purify and cleanse oneself from the stain of perversion is repentance. A repenting heart literally graces one to be presented without blemish, one to fully be used by God and to be His vessel of honor. More so, the washing of God's word will cleanse the soul of any believer and the redemptive acts of Jesus Christ with the shedding of his blood. The Word of God perfects your present of cleanses, the blood of Jesus guarantees your future of purity.

*Perversion is "the process of improperly changing something that is good."[2] Many consider perversion as sexual promiscuity or lewdness; however, perversion involves anything that changes something that is pure, clean, or holy into something immoral or diluted. A prophet must take care to remain holy and pure because perversion is destructive to the office.[3]*

---

[2] Perversion, Merriam-Webster Online Dictionary copyright © 2015 by Merriam-Webster, Incorporated. http://www.merriam-webster.com/dictionary/perversion. (accessed February 20, 2014)

[3] Dr. Larry D. Reid, *The Five-Fold Minister's Reference Book* (unknown: lulu.com, 2012), 113.

*"Also of your own selves shall men arise, speaking perverse things, to draw away disciples after them." Acts 20:30 KJV*

# I AM PROPHECY
# PRINCIPLE THREE:
# THE PRINCIPLE OF CHARACTER

> **"DEMONSTRATION, SANCTIFICATION, REVELATION, ILLUMINATION, AND MOST IMPORTANTLY MANIFESTATION; ALL FOLLOW THE MANTLE OF A PROPHET. THE KEY TO UNLOCK ONE TO THIS VAST REALM IS SUBJECTION AND SUBMISSION TO GOD'S PERFECTED WILL."**

*"Then the LORD put forth his hand, and touched my mouth. And the LORD said unto me, Behold, I have put my words in thy mouth. See, I have this day set thee over the nations and over the kingdoms, to root out, and to pull down, and to destroy, and to throw down, to build, and to plant." Jeremiah 1:9-10 KJV*

Prophets must have a life of consecration, which yields manifestation, demonstration, revelation, illumination, and sanctification to God's word and work. Jeremiah chapter 1 gives grave detail of the operations of the prophetic ministry. Insomuch Jeremiah chapter 1 informs us that a prophetic vessel's character and personality is more vital than their prophetic flow. Locked in one's lifestyle lives the key to unlock a better lifestyle for the one that is being imparted into. *2 Peter 1:5-7 ESV* gives us a clearer comprehensive perspective of this. *"For this very reason, make every effort to supplement your faith with virtue, and virtue with knowledge, and knowledge with self-control, and self-control with steadfastness, and steadfastness with godliness, and godliness with brotherly affection, and brotherly affection with love."*

# Christ-Like Character

The character of a prophetic vessel unveils manifestation not only in the life of the believer who is receiving, but for the believer that is imparting. Divine power is not merely speaking or being an oracle but having the capacity to bring manifestation and revolution to the earth realm. When we realize to be like Christ is beyond gifts, talents, and names and more revolved around His nature. When we comprehend this principle, costly mishaps will gravely diminish in the Body of Christ. Primarily as believers, we must seek to make sure our public lives are a mirror of our private lives. Looking into a cracked mirror will always give you a discombobulated imagery. Our inner man must become fulfilled so our outer man can be sustained. Satan is always looking for chemistry with the inner perils believers fight (John 14:30). Christ-Like Character is the absence of demonic chemistry; when God removes any kinsmanship of the demonic realm.

*"Beware of false prophets, which come to you in sheep's clothing, but inwardly they are ravening wolves." Matthew 7:15 KJV*

# I AM PROPHECY
# PRINCIPLE FOUR:
# MANTLES AND MANDATES

**"MANTLES ARE NEVER RELEASED IN THE PROPHETIC DIMENSION UNTIL THE MANDATE OF THE MANTLE IS RECEIVED. (THE PRINCIPLE OF THE MANTLE)"**

*"For which of you, intending to build a tower, sitteth not down first, and counteth the cost, whether he have sufficient to finish it?" Luke 14:28*

The issue in the Body of Christ is that many think that mantles (anointings, giftings, and revealed dimensions) are given/opened without a cost or a price. The mandate to every mantle is suffering and burden bearing trials; Jesus therefore stated that no man can follow me without taking up their cross. Which gives revelation that a cross is given before a crown, a burden is given before a blessing is released, and responsibilities are given before authority. The question proposed is can you carry the burden, the pain, the hurt, before you carry the blessing? Elisha the Prophet of God in 1 Kings 19:19 was plowing with 12 yoke oxen before he was given the ability to carry a mantle of the Prophet Elijah. His preparatory stage was a prerequisite for his performing stage. If Elisha could not control 12 oxen (beast of burden), harness them, train them to stay in straight rows in his father's field, maintain the yoke of the oxen, he would not been able to carry the mantle of the Prophet Elijah. Prophetic laws are revealed in his preparatory stage, which entails a prearrangement to be a burden bearer, harnessing of one's mouth, walking a circumspect lifestyle, bearing the yoke of the Lord, and grave responsibility and accountability, which is weight. If the prophetic vessel obtains a mantle and mishandles the mandate of the mantle, a suicide mission is inevitable.

# Mantles

To understand the term mantle we have to observe the prophetic ministry at a closer look. Prophets were known for wearing mantles as a sign of their calling from God. The Prophet Samuel wore a mantle (1 Sam. 15:27 KJV). 1 Kings 19:13 (KJV) speaks of a mantle where Elijah the Prophet passed or threw his mantle on Elisha the Prophet. This action between the Prophet of precession and the Prophet of succession (Elijah and Elisha) was an emblem of the passing of the prophetic ministry. The prophet's mantle was an indication of their authority and responsibility as God's chosen spokesman and oracle (2 Kings. 2:8). Like all imagery in the Old Testament, the mantle presents a visible representation of New Testament principles and revelations. The mantle also can be seen as a symbol for the anointing of the Holy Spirit whom God so graciously gives to all Christians (1 Peter 2:9, 1 Thess. 1:5-6).

Mantles are a symbol of ancient anointings and generational succession; where there is a mantle there is an antique or vintage anointing which can be traced to the first appointing of the Lord's. A prophetic legislation is found in Ps. 133, where we see the anointing of Aaron reveals a generational transference of God's power via order. Mantles are released in the same order, from the grace of a father or mother in ministry or in the gospel.

*Mantles and Mandates go hand in hand. Mandates are commands or orders given to someone. We cannot operate properly in a mantle gifting or an interchangeable term anointing (preaching, intercession, singing, etc.) without following the mandates God has set forth. As a part of the Body of Christ we must withstand persecution. The Apostle Paul in his epistle to the Hebrews states that even though Jesus was a Son, he learned obedience by the things he suffered. We must be good stewards and follow the basic principles of God by being examples for others in giving, charity, patience, long-suffering, and love.*

*"Then said Jesus unto his disciples, if any man will come after me, let him deny himself, and take up his cross, and follow me. [25]For whosoever will save his life shall lose it: and whosoever will lose his life for my sake shall find it. [26] For what is a man profited, if he shall gain the whole world, and lose his own soul? Or what shall a man gain in exchange for his soul?" Matt. 16:24-26 KJV*

*"Bear ye one another's burdens, and so fulfill the law of Christ." Galatians 6:2 KJV*

# I AM PROPHECY
# PRINCIPLE FIVE:
# THE EXTREMITY OF GOD'S
# PROTOCOL

### "APOSTLES OBTAIN LAND, PROPHETS OBTAIN MANTLES, PASTORS OBTAIN RODS, TEACHERS OBTAIN BOOKS, AND EVANGELISTS OBTAIN FIRE."

*"And he gave some, apostles; and some, prophets; and some, evangelists; and some, pastors and teachers; [12] For the perfecting of the saints, for the work of the ministry, for the edifying of the body of Christ: [13] Till we all come in the unity of the faith, and of the knowledge of the Son of God, unto a perfect man, unto the measure of the stature of the fulness of Christ" --Ephesians 4:11-13 KJV*

The Five-fold ministry graces serve as the vehicle to transport the kingdom of God to the earth realm. Serving as the Ascension Gifts/graces of God, which each function and office serves as a key to assume a higher position. The Five-fold gifts/graces represent the mobility of the church as the end-time transit for the Body of Christ. The Apostle governs you, the Prophet guides you, the Evangelist gathers you, the Pastor guards you, and finally the Teacher grounds you. By way of these five graces, we have the right to be presented and to become the developing Bride of Christ (the church).

## The Hand of God

Having the Ascension Gifts/graces functioning in the local and global church, we have the right to groom and grow each member of the Body of Christ to do greater works than the Apostles of old. Jesus told us that "greater works shall yea do" (John 14:12). Each office is needed to complete a task and operation in the earth realm for the manifestation of God's glory and for the coming of the Lord. Operating as a hand of a human being; the five-fold Ascension Gifts/graces grants the Body of Christ to hold, to feel, to grab, and maneuver the will of God in the earth realm. Many don't understand that God has equipped the church to not only stand but to work in saving souls and equipping the believers. The hand of God literally is the five-fold ministry graces that develops, reforms, activates, and cast the net of salvation for and in the church.

*Ascension literally means "to rise or assume a higher position or rank."[4] In theology, it refers to Christ's resurrection in Acts 1. Jesus returns to the right hand of the Father, but promises the Holy Ghost with whom we can perform "greater works" (John 14:12 KJV). We know that the five-fold ministry gifts are grace-given. This means we are not qualified to receive them, but they are given out of the unmerited favor of God for the upbuilding of the Kingdom.*

## Hell's Gifts

Matthew 16:18-19 KJV gives us a deeper understanding of the Ascension Gifts stating, *"And I say also unto thee, that thou art Peter, and upon this rock I will build my church; and the gates of hell shall not prevail against it. And I will give unto thee the keys of the kingdom of heaven: and whatsoever thou shall bind on earth shall be bound in heaven: and whatsoever thou shall loose on earth shall be loosed in heaven".* With this revelatory insight Jesus unlocks an in-depth revelation that he has obtain keys that the gates of Hell cannot prevail against that which has been rendered to the church. These keys have the power to *loose* and *bind,* however; the question is proposed, how did Christ get these keys and how many keys were obtained?

---

[4] Ascension, Merriam-Webster Online Dictionary copyright © 2015 by Merriam-Webster, Incorporated http://www.merriam-webster.com/dictionary/ascension. (Accessed February 22, 2014).

1 Peter 3:19 KJV *"By which also he went and preached unto the spirits in prison."* unlocks a wonder but yet the answers to the above questions. Reading 1 Peter 3:19 we understand that Jesus went into Hell and freed captives and prisoners. The term **Hell** in the text reveals an amazing factor. There are five different terms vividly used for Hell. ***Tartarus** (Genesis 6), **Paradise** (Luke 16:19-31), **Sheol** (Psalms 88:3 and Isaiah 26:19), **The Abyss** (Revelation 20:3), **and The Lake of Fire** (Revelation 20:14-15).* Isn't it ironic and yet profound that there are Five Departments of Hell and Five Ascension Gifts? Five keys that possess the power to prevail against the Five Departments of Hell. The Apostle, Prophet, Evangelist, Pastor, and the Teacher are the five keys Christ retrieved for the edifying, flotation, defense, and prevailing of the Church. You cannot be conquered or defeated by the Agents of Hell because the Ascension Gifts were birthed in the flames of Hell. The fire nor the smoke will never be able to destroy or kill what God has ordained to ascend.

"And God hath set some in the church, first apostles, secondarily prophets, thirdly teachers, after that miracles, then gifts of healings, helps, governments, diversities of tongues." 1 Cor. 12:28 KJV

# I AM PROPHECY
# PRINCIPLE SIX:
# PARALLEL PROCESSING

## "THE PROPHETIC IS COMPASSIONATE JUDGEMENT, NO MATTER HOW DREADFUL THE PROPHECY, HOPE IS ALWAYS PRESENTED."

*"The Lord is merciful and gracious, slow to anger, and plenteous in mercy" Psalms 103:8 KJV*

Prophets and prophetic vessels house the nature of Jehovah CHEREB, "The Lord of the Sword" (Deut. 33:2 KJV) and Jehovah CHAQAQ, "The Lord The Lawgiver" (Is. 33:22 KJV). However, the Word states that Christ came not to do away with the law but to fulfill the law (Matt. 5:17 KJV) and that we are able to achieve divine standards. Christ clearly states the grace/office of the Prophet serves as a guide and a divine ordinance giver. No matter how a vessel or prophetic officiate sees the sin of a sinner, we must be mindful that God's wrath is provoked from a divine jealousy as husband is over a wife. Love is the core of the indignation of heaven; God's agape (unconditional love) is encompassed in the heart of God's judgement and wrath. God even stated by way of the Ten Commandments "I am a jealous God". We all have to take note that there's a thin line between love and hate, compassion and judgement, and mainly God's grace and God's correction. There is a parallel processing; you cannot have one without the other one. *Parallel Processing is the art of needing both entities to exist.* If you cut one entity off the other entity dies; prophetic vessels and prophets must always remember Heb. 4:12 (KJV) states that the word of God is a two edged sword. You cannot have one without the other present; a parallel processing.

# Hope and Judgement

When we begin apprehending the minor and major prophets of the canon, we constantly see God's judgement contingent upon God's people in the balance of committing themselves to him as a wife to her husband. One of the objectives of the prophetic office and/or a prophetic vessel is to turn God's people back to God when they turned afar. 2 Chr. 7:14 (KJV) tell us "If my people, which are called by my name, shall humble themselves, and pray, and seek my face, and TURN from their wicked ways; then will I hear from heaven, and will forgive their sin, and will heal their land". The prophetic office brings a turn in the life of the believer who will listen and adhere to the directives that are given.

Hope is always seen or heard in the delivery of a prophetic word; hope even encompasses a prophetic word of judgement. Col. 1:27 (KJV) supports this statement in knowing that God is our hope of glory. God loves us beyond punitive measures as He did for the children of Israel whom He gave hope; so does the prophetic word of a prophetic officiant/vessel.

*"Do not think that I came to abolish the Law or the Prophets; I did not come to abolish but to fulfill." Matthew 5:17 NASB*

*"For the whole Law is fulfilled in one word, in the statement, 'You shall love your neighbor as yourself." Galatians 5:14 NASB*

*"The great day of the Lord is near, it is near, and hasteth greatly, even the voice of the day of the Lord: the mighty man shall cry there bitterly. [15] That day is a day of wrath, a day of trouble and distress, a day of wasteness and desolation, a day of darkness and gloominess, a day of clouds and thick darkness. [16] A day of the "trumpet and alarm against the fenced cities, and against the high towers. [17] And I will bring distress upon men, that they shall walk like blind men, because they have sinned against the Lord: and their blood shall be poured out as dust, and their flesh as the dung. [18] Neither their silver nor their gold shall be able to deliver them in the day of the Lord's wrath; but the*

*whole land shall be devoured by the fire of his jealousy: for he shall make even a speedy riddance of all them that dwell in the land."*
*Zeph. 1:14-18 KJV*

# I AM PROPHECY
# PRINCIPLE SEVEN:
# THE AFTERMATH OF PAIN

**"PROPHECIES ARE IDENTICAL TO VAPORS. THEY ARE MERELY WORDS UNTIL PERSECUTION, AFFLICTION, AND PRESSURE MARRIES THE CLIMATE. IT'S NOT UNTIL HEAT IS ADMINISTERED THAT A PROPHECY WILL MANIFEST."**

*"Until the time that his word came to pass, The word of the Lord tested him." Psalms 105:19 KJV*

In today's church it's very easy to tap into the realm of superstition over the supernatural realm of God, due to our anxiety attacks and anxiousness. Believing a lie over the truth, delusion over divine, and leading over serving. In my studies God unveiled a revelation about vapors that denounced the spirit of anxiety. **A vapor refers to "a gaseous substance that is below its critical temperature, and can therefore be liquefied by pressure alone**[5] (Oxford Dictionaries)".** Many want the things of God without going through the critical temperatures of trials and test. A vapor is an intangible substance until it travels through critical temperature that frames it to be a tangible substance. This process runs parallel with the virtue called manifestation. Manifestation only inaugurates when the process of hardship is prompted. Sorrow, pain, hurt, or suffering all are the words used to make the foundation for God's realm of manifestation. Jesus himself first descended before he ascended into the place of promotion (1 Pet. 3:15 KJV). Warfare makes anxiety weary. It's in the critical temperatures of suffering God depletes anxiety and our anxiousness of its strength.

---

[5] Vapor, Oxford Dictionaries.com, copyright 2017 Oxford University Press. https://en.oxforddictionaries.com/definition/us/vapor (accessed March 21, 2017).

---

# From Tangible to Intangible

The Word (the vapor) only can manifest when it has travelled through critical temperatures. It's merely just a word until that prophecy has been tried, tested, and processed. When a prophecy has been tried in the fire, there is one manifestation, which is wholeness. As with the woman with the issue of blood (Mark 8 KJV), God's rewards are revealed when we have been found to be immovable and God-like character has been stabilized within us first. Vapors are visible but intangible without the implementation of critical temperatures. Mal. 3:10 (KJV) gives us the revelation that the test comes before the manifestation and the trial must come before the verdict. Your blessings are intangible, but good news is 'AFTER-THIS' they will become tangible.

*"Bring the whole tithe into the storehouse, so that there may be [food in My house, and test Me now in this," says the Lord of hosts, "if I will not open for you the windows of heaven and pour out for you a blessing until it overflows." Mal 3:10 NASB*

*"So that the proof of your faith, being more precious than gold which is perishable, even though tested by fire, may be found to result in praise and glory and honor at the revelation of Jesus Christ" 1 Peter 1:7 NASB*

# I AM PROPHECY
# PRINCIPLE EIGHT:
# SMART DUMMIES OR ANOINTED
# FOOLS

**"PROPHETS DO NOT ENTER THE REALM OF RATIONALIZATION WHEN PROPHESYING IN THE UNKNOWN. RELYING ON FAMILIAR LOGIC TAPS INTO BEWITCHMENT AND SORCERY."**

*"Beloved, do not believe every spirit, but test the spirits to see whether they are from God, because many false prophets have gone out into the world." 1 John 4:1 KJV*

The realm of Divine Prophetic stabilizes on carnal logic to support or assist it. Many have become bewitched and controlled by sorcery, casting spells, or manipulating words that are carnally enticed and induced. Any God-given prophetic words channels through the soulish realm of man (the mind of man) which in return can pick up the emotions and intellect (thoughts) of that man. The soul of man is composed of their emotion, will, and intellect. This brings a climacteric point to illumination. If a prophetic vessel has not been processed and transformed mentally, the danger of contaminating a divine oracle of God is liable. Many times book knowledge will pervert a word from God only to confuse or even cause a destructive path for a receiving vessel. 1 Cor. 1: 27 (KJV) says "But God hath chosen the foolish things of the world to confound the wise; and God hath chosen the weak things of the world to confound the things which are mighty." This reveals that you can be a smart dummy by compiled book knowledge that cripples the will of God or an anointed fool; one that grabs the focus and attention of the world by common knowledge as Jesus did.

*Basically, obeying God's voice is key because we know one who wins souls is wise, but at times appeared as an anointed fool in doing so.*

## Rationale vs. Divine Intelligence

It is Romans 12:2 (KJV) that states 'be ye transformed by the renewing of your mind' (soul), this is a divine understanding from heaven. Rationale is a cancer to the prophetic flow of any prophetic vessel. Rationale is leaning upon man's knowledge; (scientist, doctors, and scholars) which will never trump God's divine intelligence. It's not the job of the prophetic vessel to understand the prophecy or to lean to their own understanding. The prophetic vessel has a divine mission to execute the prophecy exactly as God is stating it, without humanistic assistance. God tells us in Is. 50:14, He will give the tongue of the learned to those who submit to his divine intelligence.

One key to accurate and effective prophetic operation is fasting. Isaiah chapter 58 calls us into the fast of the Lord. Fasting kills, denounces and diminishes, our flesh. Prophetic vessels must stay in the posture of prayer and fasting, which will overcome the perils of the carnal man (flesh). When we take carnal rationalization and try to make it divine intelligence, we become smart dummies. We must understand God's ways are not our ways, and his stance will never be our stance. Many obtain the letter of the word of God but every few tap into the spirit of God's word in totality. 2 Cor. 3:6b (KJV) tells us that "the letter killeth, but the spirit giveth life." Again, this principle gives validity to the fact that rationale will never trump divine intelligence. Things shift when you initiate the God neuron called divine intelligence. You have the opportunity to tap into witty invention that are promised to the wisdom seekers.

*"And he said unto them, This kind can come forth by nothing, but by prayer and fasting." Mark 9:29 KJV*

*"I wisdom dwell with prudence and find out knowledge of witty inventions." Proverbs 8:12 KJV*

*"Who also hath made us able ministers of the new testament; not of the letter, but of the spirit: for the letter killeth, but the spirit giveth life." 2 Corinthians 3:6 KJV*

# I AM PROPHECY
# PRINCIPLE NINE:
# REJECTION AND THE PROPHETIC

> **"THE WOMB THAT NURTURES THE PROPHETIC IS CALLED REJECTION. THE FACE OF FLINT AND A KNOWING ARE THE FIRST FEATURES CREATED IN THE WOMB OF REJECTION."**

*"For the Lord God helps Me, Therefore, I am not disgraced; Therefore, I have set My face like flint, And I know that I will not be ashamed," Isaiah 50:7 KJV*

Prophetic vessels are born by persecution and rejection. Throughout scripture we see the rejection process revealed from the prophets of old until the New Testament with Christ stating, "a prophet has not honor in his own country" (John 4:44 KJV). The true revealing of a prophecy is rejection and the art of opposed manifestation or negative confirmation. Our job as prophetic vessels are to migrate the mind of God to earth, so we stand against the grain and be controversial. The "Thy Kingdom Come Migration/Movement"[6], rejection for the believer gives a face of flint that will never show the enemy we are sweating or under thoughts of forfeiting. Rejection is fuel that says you are in the will of God when you are in God. The cancer of unresolved rejection is literally the noun and medical definition of rejection in dictionary.com that states, "to cast out or eject; vomit." "To have an immunological reaction against (a

---

[6] For more information see Ralph D. Winter, *Thy Kingdom Come! The Story of a Movement; A Church for Every People and the Gospel for Every Person by the Year 2000*, gcowe ii ed. (Pasadena, Calif.: W. Carey Library, 1995),

transplanted organ or grafted tissue)."[7] The pain of unresolved rejection is that you will always try to fit in where you are denied and constantly have anti-reactions against anything that does not fit in the perfected will of God in your life. *This may sound as a cheap antidote for rejection but the cure to rejection is to "accept" rejection. Merely accept who you are, who called you, and why you are who you are, which will be revealed when you accept who you are.*

## Negative Confirmation

There is an inverted spiritual tool that is used entitled Negative Confirmation, as I stated previously. This tool is unlocked when you *accept* the fact that you are the rejected, just as Christ was the stone that the builders rejected (Matt. 21:42 KJV). The danger of this tool is that it is mistaken as an attack and it's just that confirmation from a negative source. It's a sign that you are on track with God and the heavens. You are put on a schedule with heaven when you are attacked, mishandled, rejected, misused, abused, or overlooked. It's a sign that you are close and in a position that God is about to bless or release something to you. Serving as Satan's attack but revealed as God's signal for your life. As Job the man of Uz who was attacked because of the signal of favour that was on his life. Even 1 Cor. 16:9 informs us that adversaries always huddle around open doors.

The key of it all is that Job was entertaining this principle thoroughly throughout his life. He was adamant on comprehending his negative confirmations because they all appeared as attacks but truthfully deemed him favoured. All his attacks were ended without prophetic connotation and even

---

[7] Rejection. Dictionary.com. *Dictionary.com Unabridged.* Random House, Inc. http://www.dictionary.com/browse/rejection (accessed: January 12, 2017).

rendered to him verbatim. He had four servants that spoke these words to him "and only I ESCAPED". The term escape has the word *scape* in it which means a scene. The whole trial of Job was just a scene that told us that it was going to end well. It was negative but it was anointed to prosper us. Many times God speaks and assures our ending in our beginning.

*"Whoever does not receive you, nor heed your words, as you go out of that house or that city, shake the dust off your feet." Matthew 10:14 NASB*

*"And we know that all things work together for good to them that love God, to them who are the called according to his purpose." Romans 8:28 KJV*

# I AM PROPHECY
# PRINCIPLE TEN:
# MAN CAVES AND THEIR SECRETS

**"EVERY PROPHETIC OFFICIANT MUST BE ASSIGNED TO A CAVE (CHURCH), A RAVEN (PASTORS), AND A BROOK (A LIFE STREAM OF PURITY)."**

*"The ravens brought him bread and meat in the morning and bread and meat in the evening, and he would drink from the brook."*
*1 Kings 17:6*

The Prophet Elijah is the greatest illustration of a true prophetic officiant. The cave he was assigned was the place of restoration and rejuvenation for his whole being. A cold place, a lonely place, a place where there is one voice, which is called an echo. The place where hibernation is deemed acceptable. The cave where beast go to regain their strength and redeem their sanity. The cave where reproduction and realignment can happen. Every prophetic vessel must be assigned to a cave. The cave for prophetic officiants/vessels is called a church. The place of restoration and rejuvenation, which must not be forsaken or abandoned. Heb. 10:25 KJV "forsake not the assembly of the saints". The raven is a bird of filth and thievery, but the raven that is portrayed in 1 Kings 17 illustrates a pastor or leader with flaws, struggles, and inadequacies but has a God-given assignment to give bread. Interestingly the raven was the only bird that was assigned to Elijah, which indicates you have one leader not multiple. Which illuminates the fact that there are several instructors but few fathers. (1 Cor. 4:15 KJV).

# Divine Order

*The hazard of serving and submitting to several leaders is the aperture of a clustered personality.* As we know a legion of heads is a monster in itself and a path to self-immolation. Many believers find themselves submitting to several leaders due to their attraction to a certain attribute of the vessel or their personality. That defies divine order according to 1 Kings 17 KJV; there is a sign of only one species of bird to give bread, and that's the raven. The brook signifies a plethora of prophetic laws. Purity, value, stagnation, and familiarity are just a few. The drying of the brook brings value to what was imparted. Knowing true fathers will not always be with us, cherish the flow while you have it. Not only that perspective truth is seen but stagnation is accessible for a prophetic vessel. The brook dried up as a sign that God is stating we must stay in pursuit of Him as the deer that panteth for the water brook. The brook brings revelation that being pure is more vital than anything you do as a vessel of the prophetic; consecration is the distinction between a prophetic vessel (prophet) and a psychic or vessel of demonic prophetic. Elijah's man cave reveals that there are secrets and findings that can literally define your destiny or destroy your destiny. It's all in how you handle your man cave and the secrets in your WEAK cave.

*"Obey them that have the rule over you, and submit yourselves: for they watch for your souls, as they that must give account, that they may do it with joy, and not with grief: for that is unprofitable for you." Heb. 13:17 KJV*

# I AM PROPHECY
# PRINCIPLE ELEVEN:
# THE PATIENT

## "PROPHESY THAT ENTERS OVERZEALOUSNESS, IGNITES THE INFECTION CALLED ANXIETY".

*"Not lagging behind in diligence, fervent in spirit, serving the Lord"*
*Romans 12:11 KJV*

Overzealousness will alter anyone's future as a premature infant born before time. As believers we often try to force the prophecy and/or the Word of the Lord. Mothers of the early Pentecostal movement would always say, "If the enemy cannot stop you, he will speed you up." The danger of any vessel of God is to miss the timing of heaven, by being anxious. Philippians 4:6-7 (KJV) tells us to be anxious for nothing, but in everything, we function out of prayer and supplication. Power without knowledge and divine intelligence brings more damage than success. Power without the knowledge of patience and the skill to be approximate with the things of God will cause chaos in the life of a prophetic vessels.

## Patience for the Prophecy

The book of Judges speaks of Samson, who is the epitome of this principle a vessel that was overzealous, powerful, swift, but he was divinely ignorant to Satan's devices. He constantly out ran the wisdom of God, which jeopardized his prophecy. Too much zeal will bring devastation to your prophetic Word, rather than development to your prophetic Word. Many times believers try to force the prophecy due to impatience. This is one of the greatest failures of any believer, in trying to move in God's jurisdiction. 1 Pet. 5:10 (KJV) gives us a divine equation that suffering ignites the release of the anointing of patience. *PATIENCE IS NOT A VIRTUE IT IS AN ANOINTING.* It is not just a way you stand in your ministry but it is a way to stand in your life. Patience will forfeit your traps and your hindrances in jeopardizing your prophecy. We always state only the strong survive, but the patient not only survives the patient succeeds.

*Zeal is a "strong feeling of interest and enthusiasm that makes someone very eager or determined to do something."[8] Zeal is that ambition and drive that helps us complete tasks that we are passionate about. When it comes to the things of God, we must however, remain Spirit-led. The Spirit does not always run, sometimes it walks.*

*"Also it is not good for a person to be without knowledge, And he who hurries his footsteps errs." Proverbs 19:2 KJV*

---

[8] Zeal. Merriam-Webster Online Dictionary copyright © 2014 by Merriam-Webster, Incorporated http://www.merriam-webster.com/dictionary (Accessed February 25, 2014)

---

# I AM PROPHECY
# PRINCIPLE TWELVE:
# A CRIPPLED PROPHET

**"FEAR, DOUBT, AND UNBELIEF ARE THREE DEMONIC DISEASES THAT PARALYZE PROPHECY, IF YOU UPROOT THE TRIPLETS OF HELL YOU WILL HAVE MANIFESTATION"**

*"And without faith it is impossible to please Him, for he who comes to God must believe that He is and that He is a rewarder of those who seek Him." Hebrews 11:6 KJV*

Fear is the friendly foe of every believer; fear is derived from the word "phobia". The diabolic accommodation of fear is that it serves as the demonic realms faith, which activates demonic oppression. Fear impregnates doubt into your prophecy, which gives birth to unbelief in your prophecy. Doubt is a disease that needs to be readily cured when seen. It can be portrayed as cancer it will develop and never cease to stop the spiritual decay of a vessel of God. Doubt turns into the final stage, which is a spiritual death called unbelief or better known in today's society as an atheist or non-believer.

## The Power of Unbelief

Unbelief disables any divine working of God (Matt. 13:58 KJV). Jesus even marveled at the unbelief of the city of Nazareth (Mark 6:6 KJV). As you research the city of Nazareth, you will see that the city of Nazareth was a city of great miracles and the birthing site of many patriarchs of God. Nazareth was a patriarchal birthing place but it was also a place of poverty, lack, abjection, and deficiency. In the midst of great happenings, Nazareth was the grounds for crippling the prophetic office and any prophetic officiant. How you may ask? By their unbelief and their stance in doubt. An environment that is filled with the triplets of hell will cripple a prophetic vessel and/or any vessel that God has sent to deliver that area. A place where greatness dwelled but a place where external needs were constantly at depletion.

## Power, Love, and Sound Mind

Seems as if the modern day church is a Nazareth, a place where greatness is but external stability is not taught or caught. Therefore, the infestation of subconscious atheism is in the pews and the pulpit of today's church. We appear to believe God only to unmind this form of godliness with fear, doubt, and unbelief. The key is to overcome fear the root and alpha demonic seed at all costs. 2 Tim 1:7 (KJV) reveals the key and antidote, "For God hath not given us the spirit of fear; but of power, and of love, and of a sound mind." The Triplets of Hell (Fear, Doubt, and Unbelief) can be conquered by the divine attributes of Power, Love, and a Sound Mind (a God-mind). To become courageous to trust God for what he said, to continue to love God through the times of uncertainty, and to stay focused mentally no matter the outcome.

*"But for the cowardly and unbelieving and abominable and murderers and immoral persons and sorcerers and idolaters and all liars, their part will be in the lake that burns :with fire and brimstone, which is the second death." Revelation 21:8 NASB*

*"But he must ask in faith without any doubting, for the one who doubts is like the surf of the sea, driven and tossed by the wind. 7 For that man ought not to expect that he will receive anything from the Lord, 8 being a double-minded man, unstable in all his ways." James 1:6-8 NASB*

# I AM PROPHECY
# PRINCIPLE THIRTEEN:
# 5 SHADES OF THE PROPHETIC

**THERE ARE FIVE DIMENSIONS OF THE PROPHETIC: PROPHECY OF SCRIPTURE, THE OFFICE OF THE NEW TESTAMENT PROPHET, THE SPIRIT OF PROPHECY, THE MOTIVATIONAL GIFT OF PROPHECY, AND PROPHECY".**

*"For you can all prophesy one by one, so that all may learn and all may be exhorted" 1 Cor. 14:31 KJV*

## PROPHECY OF THE SCRIPTURE

The highest level of prophecy is the Scripture itself. The Bible declares about itself that the Word of God is a "more sure word of prophecy". II Peter 1:19-21 KJV "We have also a more sure word of prophecy... no prophecy of the scripture is of any private interpretation. For the prophecy (scripture) came not in old time by the will of man..." In other words, the Scripture is infallible, inerrant, and is worthy of our undivided attention. The Scripture cannot fail; it is untainted by human error. Scripture is a more sure word to you than seeing a vision of Jesus, hearing His audible voice, or receiving a word from a prophet. Put the Word of God first place in your daily life and make it final authority over your attitudes and affairs. Become a "Bibleholic," a "Word addict" that requires an overdose every day.

# THE OFFICE OF NEW TESTAMENT PROPHET

The second level of prophecy is the office of prophet. Amos 3:7 (KJV) "Surely the Lord God will do nothing but He revealeth His secret unto His servants the prophets." Ephesians 2:20 (KJV) "And ye are built upon the foundation of the apostles and prophets, Jesus Christ Himself being the chief cornerstone." Ephesians 3:5 (KJV) "...it is now revealed unto His holy apostles and prophets by the Spirit." Ephesians 4:11 (KJV) "And He gave some apostles; and some prophets and some evangelists; and some pastors and teachers..." In the natural, every building has both a foundation underneath and a structure on top. Apostles and prophets are the foundation laying ministries. Evangelists, pastors, and teachers are the structure building ministries. When a recognized apostle or prophet speaks "Thus saith the Lord..." it carries enormous weight in the spirit realm. A prophet's prophetic word blesses, establishes, edifies, confirms, directs, corrects, comforts, roots out, destroys, plants and builds. I Samuel 3:19-20 (KJV) "and all Israel knew that Samuel was established to be a prophet of the Lord. And Samuel grew, and the Lord was with him, and let none of his words fall to the ground."

There are also five kinds of words from a prophet. *Conformational Prophecy, Creative Prophecy, Comforting Prophecy, and Challenging Prophecy*. And finally, Correctional *or Cautioning Prophecy*. The believer who is not genuinely called to this spiritual office should never attempt to copy this anointing or move in this office.[9] However, I will give a brief overview.

1.) Conformational Prophecy is when the prophet speaks a word over you that confirms what God has already been

---

[9] Dr. Dan Cheatham, Five Levels of Prophecy
http://devotionalnet.faithsite.com/uploads/147/95649.pdf (accessed

dealing with you personally. It serves as a double witness of God's leadings or dealings in your life and gives you faith to pursue His plans for your life.[10]

2.) Creative Prophecy is when the Spirit wants to do something for you or launch something into or through your life, and it otherwise would never have happened without a creative prophetic word released over your life and into your heart. Creative prophecy is the Amos 3:7 (KJV) type of prophecy, setting in motion from scratch something God wants to do.[11]

3.) Comforting Prophecy is the Acts 21:10-11 (KJV) type of prophecy, confirming and comforting you. I must also briefly mention here that the New Testament Office of Prophet is different from the Old Testament Office of Prophet. Under the OT, only three people were anointed - the prophet, the priest, and the king. The prophet carried an enormous weight of authority and responsibility before God.[12] To comfort and encourage those on the will of God.

4.) Challenging Prophecy literally is self-explanatory. It challenges you beyond the confines of your limitations; as God did Ananias and Sapphira (Acts 5 KJV). Often this kind of prophecy deals in the heart matters (money or family). The renowned Prophet Elijah was known for

---

[10] Ibid, para 3.

[11] Ibid

[12] Ibid

this kind of prophecy. 1 Kings 17: 7-16 (KJV) speaks of the Widow of Zarephath who was challenged beyond limitations. This prophecy always ends with increase and sustainability if obeyed.

5.) Correctional and Cautioning Prophecy serves as a prophetic Word of warning or direction. Nathan the Prophet came to King David in his error with this kind of prophecy (2 Sam. 12 KJV). This type of prophecy has divine consequences attached to it.

Under the New Testament, however, all believers have anointings and the Old Testament Office of Prophet has been divided up into five callings or offices - apostle, prophet, evangelist, pastor, teacher (Eph 4:11 KJV). God no longer gives that much authority to a single office or a single man. Prophets today, who think that they carry the same authority as Old Testament prophets, set themselves up for a fall.

## MOTIVATIONAL GIFT OF PROPHECY

The next level of prophecy is found in Romans 12:6-8. This is not to be confused with the office of prophet, which is a person who is called and separated, as a five-fold minister of the Gospel, and then further separated to the anointing of a prophet. The motivational gift of prophecy is a believer who is motivated to move in the gift of "prophecy" and the "spirit of prophecy" more frequently than others. Phillip's daughters were "prophesiers" yet they weren't "prophets" like Agabus (Acts 21:8-11 KJV). In I Peter 4:10-11 (KJV) we see some believers are talented by God to move in vocal expressions.

Others are gifted to serve in more practical "hands-on" expressions. *There are three vocal motivation gifts and four practical motivation gifts in Romans 12:6-8 KJV.* One of those vocal gifts is prophesying.[13]

## PROPHECY

The fourth level of prophecy is found in I Corinthians 14:3 (KJV), "But every one who prophesies speaks to men for their strengthening, encouragement, and comfort." Some poor translations change the word "prophecy" to "preach". This is a blatant error for "preach" and "prophecy" are two entirely different Greek words. The difference between the words is two-fold: *Source and Time-Element*. The source of preaching is knowledge of God's Word. The source of prophecy is the Holy Spirit (of course, prophecy will never contradict God's Word). The time-element of preaching is accumulated knowledge over a period of time. The time-element of prophecy is "on the spot" instantaneous revelation. Prophecy is a spontaneous supernatural message from God to the believer that strengthens, encourages, and comforts. All Spirit-filled believers may move in the gift of prophecy from time to time as the Spirit wills. But note that there is no prediction, no announcement of future events, and no correction in the simple gift of prophecy.

Again 1 Co 14:3 (KJV) says that the simple gift of New Testament prophecy does only three things: strengthen, encourage, and comfort. The simple gift of New Testament prophecy is not given for prediction or correction, only edification. The believer should not attempt to speak correction or prediction over someone's life without a separation and call to the office of prophet; this is obnoxious, unscriptural, manipulative, and can be dabbling with familiar spirits.[14]

---

[13] Ibid, para 5

[14] Ibid., para 6

# SPIRIT OF PROPHECY

The final level of prophecy is what I will coin the "spirit of prophecy" from Revelation 19:10 (KJV). The "spirit of prophecy" is what comes on a preacher that gives his message extra "umph", fire, and freshness. The "spirit of prophecy" is that indefinable something that often comes on you while you're witnessing to a friend. Suddenly, you can tell you're sharing exactly what the other person needs to hear. The "spirit of prophecy" is what inspires you to tell another believer how much you appreciate them with more than just a "thank you". The "spirit of prophecy" is that indefinable something that comes on you while you're praying that causes you to "change gears". You notice that you're praying with more inspiration. The "spirit of prophecy" is what prompts you to pick up the phone and just encourage or comfort a brother or sister in the Lord. The "spirit of prophecy" is simply being inspired to speak for God! Whereas prophecy is from God to you, the "spirit of prophecy" may be from you to God or from you to another. Unlike "prophecy" which is a direct "Thus saith the Lord to you", the "spirit of prophecy" is more like "Thus saith me with more inspiration from the Spirit than usual.[15]

*"Purse love, yet desire earnestly spiritual gifts, but especially that you may prophesy." 1 Corinthians 14:1 NASB*

*"Having been built on the foundation of the apostles and prophets, Christ Jesus Himself being the cornerstone." Ephesians 2:20 NASB*

---

[15] Ibid, para 7

# I AM PROPHECY
# PRINCIPLE FOURTEEN:
# A DEFECTIVE PROPHECY

## "AS A PROPHETIC VOICE, WE MUST NEVER ALLOW CIRCUMSTANCES TO INTERFERE OR DETOUR AN ASSIGNED WORD OR DIRECTIVE PROPHECY."

*"I will meditate on Your precepts And regard Your ways." Psalms 119:15 KJV*

As prophetic vessels, we must never allow distractions to interfere with our prophetic insight and sight. When this occurs, prophetic officiants just do not have a distraction they have a deadly distraction. Deadly Distractions will not only destroy your accuracy in given a word but it has the potential to destroy the vessel you are imparting into. There is a dimension of sin that is called *amiss*, which is momentous in prophetic impartation. This level of sin can make or break a prophetic vessel. James 4:3 (KJV) tells us "Ye ask, and receive not, because ye ask amiss, that ye may consume it upon your lusts." The term amiss according to the Merriam Webster Dictionary is defined as "a mistaken way, wrongly (if you think he is guilty, you judge amiss), and astray (something had gone amiss)[16]. Oh! The poison that can be imparted when a prophetic word is operating under the auspices of this dimensional sin called amiss; a defective prophecy. The term *defect* is defined as "dysfunctional yet functional". So many are functioning yet dysfunctional or defective. Whenever there is a defect with any product, there is a recall on those items. God is calling us back to our first love to refocus us.

---

[16] Amiss. Merriam-Webster Online Dictionary copyright © 2014 by Merriam-Webster, Incorporated http://www.merriam-webster.com/dictionary/amiss. (Accessed December 1,2016

---

Being that prophetic vessels mouths are lifelines for souls as a knife in the hands of a surgeon performing open-heart surgery, the wrong move or any sudden movement can cost someone their life, paralyzation, or a state of critical condition. The wrong move, wrong tool, even the wrong support in dealing with a prophetic voice can cost someone their life as well.

## FOCUS

Proverbs 4:25 (KJV) states "Let thine eyes look right on, and let thine eyelids look straight before thee." It gives revelatory insight that we have to fix our focus on the intended purpose no matter what is presented by life or the enemy. We put our emergent trials on schedule when the assignment of God is screaming to be voiced. We are fixed on the intended purpose of heaven for the intended vessels going to heaven. No matter how frustrating or imperious a situation or matter is we must put the kingdom of heaven first. Prophetic vessels must stay focused by walking in blindness to the earth realm. The danger or releasing a defected word is heightened when deadly distractions are in the focus of the prophetic vessel or prophet. Due to the spiritual principium of 2 Cor. 5:7 (KJV) "We walk not by sight, but by faith", we must follow the spiritual legislations of heaven.

*"For my eyes are toward You, O God, the Lord; In You I take refuge; do not leave me defenseless." Psalms 141:8 NASB*

*"Let thine eyes look right on, and let thine eyelids look straight before thee. [26] Ponder the path of thy feet, and let all thy ways be established. [27] Turn not to the right hand nor to the left: remove thy foot from evil." Proverbs 4:25-27 KJV*

# I AM PROPHECY
# PRINCIPLE FIFTEEN:
# PARABOLIC PROPHECIES

**"CONSECRATION/HOLINESS, DEMONSTRATION, AND EXPERIENCE ARE THE GROUNDS TO PROPHESY".**

*"Obedient children, do not be conformed to the former lusts which were yours in your ignorance,* [15] *but like the Holy One who called you, be holy yourselves also in all your behavior;* [16] *because it is written, "You shall be holy, for I am holy." 1 Peter 1:14-16 KJV*

Consecration is identical to oxygen, without oxygen, life is nonexistent as without consecration the manifestation of God is nonexistent. So we must look at the art of consecration or holiness of any believer, you cannot obtain and maintain the gift of the third person of the triune God (the Holy Spirit/Ghost) and not be consecrated or holy. Only when prophetic vessels present their bodies as living sacrifices can they encounter true power from heaven. The first attribute of the third manifested person of God named is "holy" (the Holy Spirit/Ghost), which unlocks power. The Spirit form of God, which is HOLY. Heb. 12:14 (KJV) states "Follow peace with all men, and holiness, without which no man shall see the Lord:" Holiness in layman terms is a devoted and clean life, which gives the dexterity to SEE God. Holy is not just a word that means clean but it is a term that is visible in the life of the possessor, you can SEE holy. This goes beyond dress or apparel but seeing the manifestation of God in our everyday lives, the manifested power of God used for others lives, and ultimately to see our Lord Jesus Christ in the air as 1Thess. 4: 16-17 (KJV) tells us.

# I AM PROPHECY

A consecrated life serves not as a forced deed but it is a lifestyle. The restoring of the spirit and a renewing of the mind, which impacts the body. A prophetic vessel must sacrifice their life for the power of the manifested prophetic word. Which includes living holy and righteous. One of the unique gentlemen of the scriptures is the Prophet Ezekiel. Ezekiel the Prophet was a parabolic prophet, who is the epitome of this prophetic legislation. He was parabolic, *which means he felt and became the parable he was speaking to the people of God.* He literally felt the prophecy he was giving in his body. He went as far as to demonstrate the levels of disgrace God felt by visually demonstrating. Ezekiel displayed symbolic acts such as laying on his side 430 days (Eze. 4: 3-5), cooking with the feces of cows for the exchange of men's (Eze. 4: 12-15), shaving his head bald (Eze. 12:1-7), blindfolding himself (Eze. 12: 3-12), and so much more. He became the PROPHECY! Prophets must become the prophecy; only when prophetic vessels can say, "I am Prophecy" can they prophesy the prophecy.

Many times a prophetic vessel will experience the Word of the Lord before they can give the Word of the Lord. It's not just a common cold, it's not just cold chills, it's not just verbal slander, it's a symbolic act of God's Word. Everything we do as believers must be done in the framework of holiness (expressed worship) and divine deeds (exemplars) in order to keep demonic defilement out of our purpose and spirits. Satan is a serpent and he is desperate to find himself (sin) in a vessel of God. John 14:30 (KJV) gives clarity that Satan is searching to find himself in us to possess or oppress us to fight the will of God or hinder the will of God in us.

Consecration not only serves as a lifestyle of purity and peace but it serves as a lifestyle of worship and bodily expressions. Being one that worships God is seen not just in our charismatic behaviors in our institution's called church, but in our daily affairs. We become expressionists; I have a rhetorical question for you Heb 12:14 (KJV) says 'Be ye holy for I AM holy.' I ask you is this verse saying BE holy (become holy) or BE (show/express) HOLY?

*Consecrate means "to devote irrevocably to the worship of God."[17] Prophetic vessels must devote their lives wholeheartedly to God. This cover the three areas of subjection; which are thought, action, and speech. Every thought, action, or word must be done with God in mind. Does this glorify God? Does this help or hinder the move of the Kingdom?*

*"No one who abides in Him sins; no one who sins has seen Him or knows Him [7]Little children, make sure no one deceives you; the one who practices righteousness is righteous, just as He is righteous; [8]the one who practices sin is of the devil; for the devil has sinned from the beginning. The Son of God appeared for this purpose, to destroy the works of the devil. [9]No one who is born of God practices sin, because His seed abides in him; and he cannot sin, because he is born of God. [10]By this the children of God and the children of the devil are obvious: anyone who does not practice righteousness is not of God, nor the one who does not love his brother." 1 John 3:6-10 NASB*

---

[17] "Consecrate." Merriam-Webster Online Dictionary copyright © 2014 by Merriam-Webster, Incorporated http://www.merriam-webster.com/dictionary/consecrate. (Accessed February 28, 2014.)

# I AM PROPHECY
# PRINCIPLE SIXTEEN:
# AUTHORS AND ILLUSTRATORS

## "EVERY WORD HAS TWO SIDES
## - WHO SPEAKS IT AND WHO WRITES IT."

*"For the word of God is living and active and sharper than any two-edged sword, and piercing as far as the division of soul and spirit, of both joints and marrow, and able to judge the thoughts and intentions of the heart." Hebrews 4:12 KJV*

The Bible, some call it the Canon, others the Septuagint, the Torah, the Midrash, primarily known as the Word of the Lord functions as the highest stratum and pinnacle of heaven. The power of the word of the Lord has a multiplicity of effects, being able to cut but heal, bind or liberate, curse or bless, blind or give sight, lame or cause to walk, divide or multiply, increase or decrease, promote or demote. The Word of God is the only agent deemed to have the potency to separate the soul and spirit of a person. Heb 4:12 (KJV) gives us many facets of the aptitude of the Word of God, from dividing the soul and spirit of a human, having the efficacy of separating joints and bone marrow, to judging the heart of a man. Psalms even tells us that the Word of God takes precedence even over the name of Christ (Ps. 138:2 KJV).

## Logos and Rhema

Hebrews tells us that the word of God is like a two-edged sword, which has the capability to divide and multiply. The power of the sacred writ is that the word of God is revealed in having two sides. Those sides are called rhema and logos. Rhema the spoken word of God and Logos the written word of God. Many try to receive RHEMA (*the spoken word*) without receiving LOGOS (*the written word*). The voice of the spoken Word will never be louder than the voice of the written Word; they are in harmony with each other. God will never allow a spoken word to go forth without allowing it to synchronize with His written Word.

Logos is the only promising Word from God that will never perish or wither away. God tells us everything will pass away but His WORD (Matt. 24:35 KJV). A word or phrase that is spoken cannot be patented or copyrighted until it has been written. Copies cannot be made, license cannot be registered, or ownership cannot be granted. That's why Hab. 2:2 (KJV) tell us to write the vision, due to the fact that a word has the potential to materialize when it has been written and then spoken. Illustration comes when it is written, you can see the manifestation of a word when it is written. Prophetic words must originate from the framework of the Word of God before it is portrayed by a prophetic vessel.

*The written word or Logos of God is what can keep us. In His Word, we find His promises as well as His instructions for daily living. The Word convicts, energizes, and shapes our lives. When spoken (Rhema) the manifestation of God's promises starts to shift into your reality.*

## The Illustrator

Where there is an author there is an illustrator. According to Hebrews 12:2 KJV, the author of Hebrews gives us a principle that is profoundly stated. *"Looking unto Jesus the author and finisher of our faith; who for the joy that was set before him endured the cross, despising the shame, and is set down at the right hand of the throne of God."*

Cognitive Science says that words that are accompanied with pictures are called mental images. *Sanford Encyclopedia of Philosophy* states, *"mental imagery is (varieties of which are sometimes colloquially referred to as "visualizing," "seeing in the mind's eye," "hearing in the head," "imagining the feel of," etc.) is quasi-perceptual experience; it resembles perceptual experience, but occurs in the absence of the appropriate external stimuli."*[18] Being that we are God-Like in cognition and physicality, what we say with our mouths we will see in our mind that will become a reality in our hands.

As prophetic vessels we must grasp the principle that Jesus is the author of our faith but we are the illustrators of our manifestation. Christ wrote and spoke with His creative power but it's our job to see and make it. Imagination will become manifestation in the hands of a prophetic vessel that possess faith. It all starts with a word because faith cometh by hearing and hearing by the word of the Lord (Romans 10:17 KJV).

*"And take the helmet of salvation and the sword of the Spirit, which is the Word of God." Ephesians 6:17 ESV*

*"Now He said to them, "These are My words which i spoke to you while I was still with you, that all things which are written about Me in the Law of Moses and the Prophets and the Psalms must be fulfilled." [45]Then He opened their minds to understand the Scriptures". Luke 24:44-45 NASB*

---

[18] The Stanford Encyclopedia of Philosophy
https://plato.stanford.edu/entries/mental-imagery/ (Accessed May 31, 2017)

# I AM PROPHECY
# PRINCIPLE SEVENTEEN:
# DILATED EYES

> **"A Prophet of God must possess SEVEN eyes in the spirit-realm. Only when all eyes are open can a prophetic vessel see beyond sight but in divine insight."[19]**

*"And the spirit of the Lord shall rest upon him, the spirit of wisdom and understanding, the spirit of counsel and might, the spirit of knowledge and of the fear of the Lord; [3] And shall make him of quick understanding in the fear of the Lord: and he shall not judge after the sight of his eyes, neither reprove after the hearing of his ears." Isaiah 11: 2-3 KJV*

The "Seven Spirits" represent the sevenfold ministry of the Spirit as depicted in the Book of Isaiah. As it is written: "The Spirit of the LORD shall rest upon him, the Spirit of wisdom and understanding, the Spirit of counsel and might, the Spirit of knowledge and of the fear of the LORD, and He will delight in the fear of the Lord." (Isaiah 11:2-3 NASB). Including the Spirit of the Lord, and the Spirits of *wisdom*, of *understanding*, of *counsel*, of *might*, of *knowledge* and of *fear of the LORD*, here are represented the seven Spirits, which are before the throne of God. This is a reference to the lamb in Revelation 5:6 (KJV) which relates to the Seven Spirits which first appear in Revelation 1:4 (KJV) and are associated with Jesus who holds them along with seven stars. Biblically there are seven graces ("charisma") of Romans 12:6-8 (KJV) that reflect the seven spirits of God. The Holy Spirit manifests in humankind through these graces, reflecting the seven spirits of the Holy Spirit. *The seven graces are: 1) insight (prophecy); 2) helpfulness (service*

---

[19] "Isaiah 11: 2-3 KJV

*or ministries); 3) instruction (teaching); 4) encouragement; 5) generosity (giving); 6) guidance (leadership); and 7) compassion.* This agrees with Isaiah 11:2-3 (KJV) if "the Spirit of the Lord" is recognized as categorical and "the delight in the fear of the Lord" is added.

## Dilating the Eyes

A Prophet of God cannot operate in the spirit of the Holy Spirit that teaches all things and do not possess the seven eyes of the spirit of God. In visiting the ophthalmologist (eye specialist) the first step to an eye examination is to dilate the eyes. The term dilate literally means to *widen* or *spread*, to *increase*, and/or *broaden*. Many misinterpret this process due to the aftereffects of temporary blindness. This process is the comprehensive dilated eye exam, which gives the eye specialist the ability to view inside the eye. Eye dilation allows more light to enter the eye the same way opening a door allows light into a dark room. However; eye dilation literally opens the eye pupils which puts the eyes at a better advantage in seeing. Doesn't seem true due to the fact your eyes are not normally in a dilated position. It's in the posture of God opening your eyesight as he did the Apostle Paul in Acts 9:12 (KJV), that a prophetic vessel will enter divine sight which opens all seven eyes of the spirit of the Lord.

The mishap in the office of the prophet is that many prophetic vessels possess very few eyes of the Holy Spirit. To an effective prophetic voice in the kingdom the eyes of the Holy Spirit must be opened and functioning in order to guide the church to the coming of the Lord. The seven eyes of the Prophetic Realm are needed more so than ever for the church to function in the full capacity that she needs to be in for the coming of the Lord. It's only when a prophetic vessel asks God to dilate the seven eyes of the spirit, that true insight is given.

*"As for you, the anointing which you received from Him abides in you, and you have no need for anyone to teach you; but as His anointing teaches you about all things, and is true and is not a lie, and just as it has taught you, you abide in Him." 1 John 2:27 NASB*

*"But the Helper, the Holy Spirit, whom the Father will send in My name, He will teach you all things, and bring to your remembrance all that I said to you." John 14:26 NASB*

# I AM PROPHECY
# PRINCIPLE EIGHTEEN:
# IMPULSIVE PROPHETS

**"THE SEAT OF YOUR EMOTIONS AS A PROPHETIC VESSEL IS THE ENEMY OF YOUR VOICE. EMOTIONS CAN MAKE A PROPHETIC VOICE HOARSE"**

*"We are destroying speculations and every lofty thing raised up against the knowledge of God, and we are taking every thought captive to the obedience of Christ." 2 Corinthians 10:5 KJV*

The soulish realm is the most complex component of mankind. The soul governs our emotion, will, and intellect, which governs our deeds. Toxic emotions (fruits of the flesh/carnality) all hinder the clarity of a prophetic voice. A primary objective of a prophetic voice is to master his/her emotions, so he/she can be heard clearly by humanity and hell. There is nothing worse than a hoarse psalmist, so is it in the prophetic realm. There is nothing worse than an over-emotional prophetic vessel. As an over-emotional prophetic vessel when your emotions are not stable, you speak as a mad man/woman. You are very indecisive and your vision becomes distorted with your emotions. Your emotions become poison to your divine mission. Only when emotions are controlled you can unlock and mature your destiny and purpose in GOD.

## Dangers of Impulsivity

We see this infection with King Saul of 1 and 2 Samuel, he is dancing and prophesying with the company of the prophets and soon after he is making an emotional decision with rebelling towards the will of God in killing the King of Agag (1 Sam. 15 KJV). Via this text you will see that God rejected him thereafter due to the insuppressible actions of his carnality. King Saul went from prophesying with the company of prophets to the consulting of a necromancer of Endor (1 Sam. 28 KJV). Oh, the places your emotions will take you if you do not master them promptly and properly. There is a term in behavioral literature that defines the actions of King Saul--**IMPULSIVE**. Impulsivity is a neurological construct that makes one act on a whim, displaying a behavior characterized by little or no forethought, reflection, or consideration of the consequences.[20] This defines a premature expression which impedes long-term goals and ultimately obstructs prophecy.

King Saul operated under a prophetic mantle or anointing but impulsive behavior (becoming emotional) he made a intertemporal choice which caused him the kingdom that God blessed him with. The bible says King Saul failed twice 1 Sam. chapters 13-15; the same toxic emotion of rebellion caused him to become impulsive twice which caused him to mishandle the anointing and blessings of God. Toxic emotions will become a cancer to the gifting and anointing God has graced any prophet, prophetic vessel, or believer. Which in turn will cause the forfeiting of destiny. We must do all things in prayer and supplication (Phil. 4:6). Only in prayer and much thought can you enter destiny strategically.

---

[20] "Impulsive" wikipedia.org .https://en.wiktionary.org/wiki/impulsive. (Accessed January 15, 2017)

*"A fool always loses his temper, but a wise man holds it back."*
*Proverbs 29:11 NASB*

*"He who is slow to anger has great understanding, but he who is quick-tempered exalts folly." Proverbs 14:29 NASB*

# I AM PROPHECY
## PRINCIPLE NINETEEN:
## FRUSTRATION OR ACCOUNTABILITY

## "PROPHECY SHOULD NEVER BE PRESENTED AS ENTERTAINMENT BECAUSE IT IS A BURDEN FROM THE LORD"

*"For you will no longer remember the oracle of the Lord, because every man's own word will become the oracle, and you have perverted the words of the living God, the Lord of hosts, our God. [37] Thus you will say to that prophet. 'What has the Lord answered you?' and 'What has the Lord spoken?' [38] For if you say, 'The oracle of the Lord!' surely thus says the Lord, 'Because you said this word, "The oracle for the Lord!" I have also sent to you, saying, "You shall not say, 'The oracle of the Lord!"' Jeremiah 23:36-38 KJV*

Jeremiah the Weeping Prophet states the Word of the Lord is a burden, a ball and chain, a weary load, an agony. From the beginning of time to the very present animating of existence the word of the Lord has been presented as an adiposity. From the Prophets of Old to the Apostles of the New Testament, several ask the million-dollar question how is the Word of the Lord a burden? The frustration that comes with releasing a word that often times is rejected and mishandled. Many aspects are locked in the Word of the Lord; the lives of the receiver, the listener, and even the giver are hanging in the balance between life and death. What is frustration at its core? *Merriam-Webster defines frustration as "a: to balk or defeat in an endeavor. b : to induce feelings of discouragement".[21]* Sometimes discouragement is accompanied by discomfort. To induce the feeling of discouragement and discomfort. Prophetic vessels

---

[21] "Frustration". Merriam-Webster Online Dictionary copyright © 2015 by Merriam-Webster, Incorporated. https://www.merriam-webster.com/dictionary/frustration. (Accessed January 18. 2017)

must be detached from their emotions. The overwhelming feelings are merely just feelings.

Frustration comes when there is an endeavor expected to be completed. Its inevitable frustration will come when accountability is present, but what is the fore running attribute? Is it the endeavor or the fact the endeavor has stipulations?

## Burdens and Blessings

In today's church we have made the prophetic dimension and prophecy overall a joke and a sitcom that we watch. Life is found in the words of the prophet; your future can be released by one word. Prosperity is locked in the jaws of the prophetic voice. Today, believe in the voice of your prophetic vessel and prosperity can be unlocked over your life. The **BURDEN** can be metamorphosed to a **BLESSING** if the receiver will just **BELIEVE.** The danger of releasing prophetic words are not just the articulation of the word, but the burden of who you have to speak to. The amount of pressure that heaven has on your back is like a elephant on the back of an infant. Who can feel the pain of the vessel that God has anointed to carry this word and this burden. Is it frustration you feel or is it accountability? The dependency heaven has on you to release a word that will shift the earth realm. Many times frustration comes not from anger but the fact that there is friction, there is a movement that is happening and you have to oblige to it. Either you break or bend, you die or live, you sit or stand, but whatever you do you have to release. Heaven is counting on you.

*"They rose early in the morning and went out to the wilderness of Tekoa; and when they went out, Jehoshaphat stood and said, "Listen to me, O Judah and inhabitants of Jerusalem, put your trust in the Lord your God and you will be established. Put your trust in His prophets and succeed." 2 Chronicles 20:20 KJV*

# I AM PROPHECY
# PRINCIPLE TWENTY:
# WORDS AND WORLDS

> **"A PROPHET'S MOUTH CAN CAUSE MORE DAMAGE THAN A NUCLEAR BOMB IN THE TIME OF WAR. A NUKE CAN KILL A NATION/REGION/GENERATION BUT A PROPHET'S MOUTH CAN KILL GENERATIONS UNTO THE FOURTH GENERATION"**

*"Then the Lord passed by in front of him and proclaimed, "The Lord, the Lord God, compassionate and gracious, slow to anger, and abounding in lovingkindness and truth; 7 who keeps lovingkindness for thousands, who forgives iniquity, transgression and sin; yet He will by no means leave the guilty unpunished, visiting the iniquity of fathers on the children and on the grandchildren to the third and fourth generations." Exodus 34:6-7 KJV*

Mastery of your mouth and words as prophetic vessels is a necessity within the operations as a prophetic vessel. Mastery of one's emotions will swiftly monitor speaking nonsensical in an irrational climate that can be a moment of regret in the future. God is the God of generations when He looks in the direction or speaks in the direction of an individual; He sees not the individual but the generation and the generations of the individual to come.

Therefore, what is released verbally by God's mouthpiece (His prophets) affect everything that is connected to that individual even going into the supernatural realm. When prophetic vessels speak they speak from eternity which deals with generations to come. Rom. 4:17 (KJV) states, "that we speak those things that are not as though they are, which can move from the realm of curses to the realm of blessings dependent upon the vessel that is speaking." God never wastes words, anything spoken encompasses heavens creative power to fulfill and manifest in the earth realm. Life and Death lives and resides in the mouth of a prophetic vessel and primarily one that serves God (Prov. 18:21 KJV)

## New Levels Equals New Languages

It's not until we understand that the cliché new level new devil is merely elementary revelation we will continue having verbal mishaps. It's not new devil but new language. New level, new language. Your speech and your dialogue changes upon your maturation. Heb. 11:3 (KJV) illuminates a profound law that by the words of God were worlds are framed.

When prophetic vessels understand the system of communication in governing words then and only then can they summon the kingdom of God to the earth realm. The American vocabulary is made up of vowels (*a, e, i, o, u*) and consonants, which are all other letters outside of the 'five'. It is literally impossible to speak without a vowel present in a word. Vowels build the skeleton of words, the word vowels has the root term *vow*, which literally means to breathe from the larynx. The preposition is until a prophet or prophetic vessel comprehends the value of God breathing through them, which enables them to speak, he/she cannot speak on the behalf of God. Prophetic vessels must inhale what God exhales in order to speak the words of God, which creates the worlds of God. The term vow also is defined to pay a price or pledge. There is no way a prophetic word is released and not paid for by the one that releases it and the one that receives it. Every prophetic vessel and prophet must **WATCH THEIR MOUTH!**

*"And he went up from thence unto Bethel: and as he was going up by the way, there came forth little children out of city, and mocked him, and said unto him, Go up, thou bald head; go up, thou bald head.* [24] *And he turned back, and looked on them, and cursed them in the name of the Lord. And there came forth two she bears out of the wood, and tare forty and two children of them." 2 Kings 2:23-24 KJV*

*"For in many things we offend all. If any man offend not in word, the same is a perfect man, and able also to bridle the whole body.* [3] *Behold, we put bits in the horses' mouths, that they may obey us; and we turn about their whole body.* [4] *Behold also the ships, which though they be so great, and are driven of fierce winds, yet are they turned about with a very small helm, whithersoever the governor listeth.* [5] *Even so the tongue is a little member, and boasteth great things. Behold, how great a matter a little fire kindleth!* [6] *And the tongue is a fire, a world of iniquity: so is the tongue among our members, that it defileth the whole body, and setteth on fire the course of nature; and it is set on fire of hell.* [7] *For every kind of beasts, and of birds, and of serpents, and of things in the sea, is tamed, and hath been tamed of mankind:* [8] *But the tongue can no man tame; it is an unruly evil, full of deadly poison.* [9] *Therewith bless we God, even the Father; and therewith curse we men, which are made after the similitude of God.* [10] *Out of the same mouth proceedeth blessing and cursing. My brethren, these things ought not so to be." James 3:2-10 KJV*

*"A wholesome tongue is a tree of life: but perverseness therein is a breach in the spirit." Proverbs 15:4 KJV*

# I AM PROPHECY
# PRINCIPLE TWENTY-ONE:
# WHEN TEARS PROPHESY

**"A PROPHET'S TEARS ARE BETTER ON THE GROUND OF THE EARTH, THAN IN THE HAND OF GOD. A WOUNDED PROPHET IS DANGEROUS."**

*"The boastful shall not stand before Your eyes; You hate all who do iniquity." Psalms 5:5 KJV*

A prophet known for his tears is Jeremiah the weeping prophet. The many difficulties he encountered as we read his writings in the scriptures, Jeremiah and the book of Lamentations. Jeremiah chapters 21-38 gives credence to the terrifying times Jeremiah the Prophet lived in. Times great nations were struggling for control of the world, the powerful Assyrian Empire was slowly dying, Babylon was becoming the superpower of that time, and Egypt wanted to keep its crown as the world's superpower for 1000 years. The pain of it is that God's people (Judah) was residing between Babylon and Egypt. This caused Jeremiah the Prophet to weep due to the sins of God's people. Gods people of that time had succumb to the pagan rituals of the surrounding nations. By turning on God, preaching and precepts fell on deaf ears, and the people of God had become so corrupt that they even came against the Prophet of God Jeremiah. Jeremiah became a wounded, weary, weeping prophet.

# The Anatomy of Tears

Jeremiah was wounded by their acts towards God. The dilemma is a wounded prophet or prophetic vessel ignites the nature of Jehovah Gmolah (the Lord of Recompense) into the earth realm. The nature of God of repayment and judgement. Jehovah Gmolah abides and dwells in the tears of a distressed prophetic vessel or believer in general. Tears are biblically recorded as data for God to use for us, against the enemy that stands against us or the valley that stands between us and God (Ps 56:8 KJV). The anatomy of tears are locked into three dimensions:

**1. Basal**
**2.Reflexive**
**3. Psychological**

Each tear is designed to support the eye of the host at all cost. *Basal tears* lubricate the eye from drought or drying out, *Reflexive tears* are the tears that protect the eyes when bacterial or a foreign element is or has entered the eye. *Psychological tears* are called prophetic tears; these tears hold the very DNA of the host's subconscious. The shortest bible verse is found in John 11:35 (KJV) where we read the famous text that says "Jesus wept". Psychological tears of a prophetic stance is where God reveals his next mission via the release of tears. The release of the next of God is seen in Christ stating "Lazarus is not dead he is sleeping". The next move is seen and immediately next is no longer next; NEXT becomes NOW. A very present help in the time of trouble is prompted in the heavenlies (Ps. 46:1 KJV). It's in these dimensional tears a prophetic vessel/officiant can end drought, war against the demonic realm, and prophetically decree and declare.

## Water to Weapons

Just as Christ wept so does believers, however; when a believer cries from the soul or the realm of the supernatural (psychological tears), tears literally metamorphoses from water to weapons. Supernatural distress calls are made when the righteous cries from the uttermost of their being. DON'T MAKE ME CRY! Ps 34:17 (KJV) states "when the righteous cries (the prophetic vessel) it moves God to move for the vessel who has cried." Your tears are weapons of power when you are called to the realm of the prophetic, use them wisely. That's how we stand on the words of the Psalmist that said, "those that sow in tears, shall reap in joy" (Ps. 126:5 KJV). Prophetic vessels tears speak when the voice of the prophetic vessel is silenced.

## Tears Can Speak

One of the most eminent principles of tears is that tears are not just weapons they can possess the prayers of the righteous. Ps. 56:8 KJV says "Thou tellest my wanderings put thou my tears into thy bottles: are they not in thy book?" With this powerful text we see that God literally records your tears, tears in a book. Only words belong in books, and liquids belong in bottles. Tears speak, tears *Heb. shabach* (to shout unto God with the voice of joy)[22], tears can prophecy.

*"Do not touch My anointed ones, And do My prophets no harm."*
*Psalms 105:15 KJV*

*"Never take your own revenge, beloved, but leave room for the wrath of God, for it is written, "Vengeance is Mine, I will repay," says the Lord." Romans 12:19 NASB*

---

[22]"Shabach" http://biblehub.com/hebrew/7623.htm (Accessed March 24, 2017)

---

# I AM PROPHECY
# PRINCIPLE TWENTY-TWO:
# THE AMPHIBIAN SPIRIT
## (DIVINE PROPHETIC OR DEMONIC PROPHETIC)

**"THE CALLING OF CREDIT/DEBIT CARDS NUMBERS, ADDRESSES, OR EVEN NAMES DOES NOT DENOTE TRUE PROPHETIC OPERATION BUT EVIDENCE OF TRUE REPENTANCE DOES."**

*"Repent, for the kingdom of heaven is at hand." Matthew 3:2 KJV*

The realm of the prophetic has been gravely misunderstood and has developed a complex projection within the church arena. Many denote several vessels as prophets, prophetic vessels, or believers that encompass the prophetic operations of God by mere external observation. However, one should never identify a prophet or prophetic vessel solemnly on the external attributes nor merely external observation alone. In true scriptural context prophecy is foretelling or forthtelling of a futuristic event that has not occurred yet. Calling physical miscellaneous items is not categorized as prophecy it is columned under the word of knowledge, which can tap into the realm of the demonic if enticed with carnal motive. 2 Chr. 18 (KJV) speaks of a divine legislation that is very imperative to comprehend, it speaks of demonic prophetic. The summoning of a lying wonder spirit is sanctioned by the priest and anti-prophets of King Ahab because King Ahab wanted to hear pleasant prophecies even though he obtained a corrupt character. King Ahab rejected the word of the Lord from God's true Prophet Micaiah and honored the demonic prophetic from his anti-prophets.

# Frogs, Toads, and Salamanders (Amphibians)

We see the operation of Demonic Prophetic in the New Testament. In the book of Revelations 16:13 (KJV) we observe three unclean spirits in the frame of FROGS coming out of the mouth of the dragon (Satan), the beast (Anti-Christ), and the false prophet. Each frog (unclean spirit) worked miracles and performed upon the same framework as that of the spirit of God. They released blessings, they released miracles, and prophecies only to recruit for the battle of the great day of God Almighty. This is called the **AMPHIBIAN SPIRIT**; an amphibian can function in the aquated kingdom and the terrestrial kingdom (Frogs, Toads, and Salamanders are all amphibians.) *These unique creatures have the capacity to live on land and in water; in the Greek the term amphibian derived from the term amphibious meaning "living a double life."* When a prophet, prophetic vessel, or a believer tries to live a double life, they activate the amphibian spirit in their life. James 1:8 (KJV) gives us further revelation that a double-minded posture makes anyone unstable.

As previously stated an amphibian can live in two different habitats land and water, which has spiritual symbolism of spirit and flesh. The Apostle Paul tells us in Rom. 8:1 (KJV) that we walk not after the flesh, but after the spirit. No man can serve two masters (Matt. 6.24 KJV), true prophetic stance calls the people of God to a divine revolution and divine alignment.

# Pleasant Prophecies

The Amphibian Spirit encompasses pleasant prophecies that will seduce, deceive, misguide, and cause a forfeiting destiny. Pleasant prophecies are not primarily God if the receiver carries corrupt character as King Ahab did. *If seeing miscellaneous commodities stand as the core defining of prophecy within the church arena, we have missed the mark drastically.* Authentic prophetic vessels and God's ordained prophet's demand repentance, the turning of a man's heart towards God (2 Chr. 7:14 KJV). Biblical history gives us in-depth detail of the operations of witches, warlocks, wizards, and sorcerers from Jannes and Jambres (Ex 7:10-12 KJV) to the wizardries of Acts (Acts 19 KJV), everyone embedded in demonic functioning recorded biblically wanted self-gain and wealth. Therefore, the revelation is birthed that psychic's, wizards, and witches see *on* you but prophet's see *in* you. **Psychics see your desires as a Prophet of God sees your purpose or destiny.** *Authentic prophet's concern is never geared to external appeasing but primarily the internal state of a vessel.* Which entails the condition of one's heart, the renewing of one's mind, turning from a sinful nature, and perfecting the will of God in one's life. Remember this example, demonic prophetic sees your house; divine prophetic sees your heart! Choose ye this day whom ye will serve (Josh. 24:15 KJV)!

*"And saying, "The time is fulfilled, and the kingdom of God is at hand; repent and believe in the gospel." Mark 1:15 KJV*

# I AM PROPHECY
# PRINCIPLE TWENTY-THREE:
# THE ECLIPSE PRINCIPLE

## "PROPHET'S MUST QUICKLY GRASP THE PHILOSOPHY OF ECLIPSING AND EXPOSING BEFORE PROPHETIC MATURATION IS REACHED."

*"Brethren, even if anyone is caught in any trespass, you who are spiritual, restore such a one in a spirit of gentleness; each one looking to yourself, so that you too will not be tempted." Galatians 6:1 KJV*

The prophetic realm and ministry unlocks the ability to examine the weaknesses and issues in the Body of Christ. Seeing into the lives of individuals is powerful yet dangerous if mishandled. A mishandled component before prophetic maturation is the potentiality to know when to eclipse or expose an area of weakness and detriment. God curses the vessel that instigates premature exposure, exposing a Noah and a Herod are two different dynamics that can potentially have congruent endings with two different intentions. The power exercised by John the Baptist the greatest prophet of all time, Luke 3:19-20 KJV ("[19] But Herod the tetrarch, being reproved by him for Herodias his brother Philip's wife, and for all the evils which Herod had done, [20] Added yet this above all, that he shut up John in prison.") in exposing King Herod for the act of incest, is not the power exercised by Ham the Son in exposing his father's nakedness (Noah) in Gen. 9:22 (KJV) which rest on the same foundation of incest. "And Ham, the father of Canaan, saw the nakedness of his father, and told his two brethren without."

# Noah vs. Herod

Noah needed to be eclipsed by his son Ham, while Herod needed to be exposed by John the Baptist. The term *eclipse* means *"the obstruction of the light, intervention from exposure."*[23] The benefit of this principle is both Ham and John the Baptist had harsh endings but each individual act was birthed from two opposing and opposite spirits. Ham's objective was to sabotage Noah's success, while John the Baptist objective was to reprimand the spirit of incest in Herod.

Comprehending this principle will reveal that Noah can curse you unto your fourth generations for premature exposure, while Herod can bind and behead you to enhance a kingdom revolution. However; Herod's exposure was for divine elucidation for the holistic edification for the Body of Christ, but Noah's exposure was to damage and defile the representation of the Body of Christ. The divine craftsmanship of covering and revealing, eclipsing and exposing is a gift of understanding timing. A prophetic officiant/vessel must be in harmony with heaven beyond performance of the prophetic gifts but in relationship with God to understand the timing of usage for the gift.

---

[23] "Eclipse". eclipse. Dictionary.com. *Collins English Dictionary - Complete & Unabridged 10th Edition.* HarperCollins Publishers. http://www.dictionary.com/browse/eclipse (Accessed January 16, 2017)

# The Eclipse Principle

Studies show that an Eclipse Season happens twice a year and usually lasts on an average of 34.5 days. This season is when the moon moves between the sun and earth, which blocks the sun's illumination and in return casts a shadow upon the earth. Some physicist believe this natural act can support the isothermal layer of the earth, which is the layer that absorbs most of the Sun's ultraviolet radiation, which causes cancer and other incurable diseases. This is called a Solar Eclipse; it's a powerful natural phenomenon. We are to respond to situations and hardships as the moon does for the earth and the sun. The moon serves as an intercessor for the earth and the sun. Standing in between me and thee, hurt and help, restoration and dissolution. God calls us to eclipse (hide) another man's issues, inadequacies, and downfalls.

The Sons of Sceva (Acts 3 KJV) exposed and erected a demonic entity that subdued them; they tried to cast out what they were sleeping and wrestling with.

Exposure where intercession is needed will *deactivate* the potential of victory for the vessel who receives and *activate* defeat for the vessel who imparts. We are called to elevate and restore such a one (Gal 6:1 KJV) in their decline, no matter the frailty of the individual. Eclipsing a man's weakness will restore the man to wholeness; remember God's grace is sufficient for us all (2 Cor. 12:9 KJV).

*"And above all things have fervent charity among yourselves: for charity shall cover the multitude of sins." 1 Peter 4:8 KJV*

# I AM PROPHECY
# PRINCIPLE TWENTY-FOUR:
# THE LUCIFERIAN PRINCIPLE

## "PRIDE IS AN ETERNAL SIN, CREATED IN THE THRONE ROOM OF HEAVEN; COMPOSED BY LUCIFER HIMSELF."

*Pride goeth before destruction, and an haughty spirit before a fall.*
*Proverbs 16:18 KJV*

One of the foundational sins of humanity is the spirit of pride. There are several scriptures that brings this revelation to transparency primarily 1 John 2:16 (KJV), which states, "For all that is in the world, the lust of the flesh, and the lust of the eyes, and the PRIDE of life, is not of the Father, but is of the world". Pride stands as one of the originating illegal acts of heaven and earth. From millennial prophetic vessels to patriarchal/matriarchal of the prophetic ministry. Many have been infected by this incurable disease, many have died from this incurable disease, even annihilated generations by this incurable disease. The soul disease called PRIDE has taken many. Like a loose strand of hair on the epidermis of skin; it's agile, airy, and agitating but hard to identify. You can have this soul disease and not know you are infected, because it accompanies success, blessings, and health.

# Lucifer's Demise

Isaiah chapter 14 (KJV) unveils a wonder name Lucifer the mighty anointed cherub of the Lord; whose name is translated in Hebrew as "helel,"[24] which means brightness. In Isaiah 14: 12-14 (KJV) the Eagle Eyed Prophet (Isaiah) speaks of the celestial wonder who we see is the chief of Praise and Worship of the third dimension of heaven (2 Cor. 12: 2-4 KJV). The third dimension is known as the dwelling place of God Himself. Who is asked the million-dollar question by God "How are you fallen from heaven, O Day Star, son of Dawn"? Lucifer is an interchangeable name for Satan, who serves as the supreme chief officiating officer of this world's-system. This passage of scripture (Is. 14: 12-14 KJV) goes beyond the confines of humanistic comprehension, this text marks the beginning of one of the founding sins in the universe and the very fall of Lucifer/Satan in the primeval, sinless spheres before the creation of man.

## The Luciferian Principle

We see this same motif in Ezekiel 28:11-19 (KJV), where Lucifer/Satan's appearance is described in depth, his signet of perfection and beauty. Only to find PRIDE in his heart, which corrupted his wisdom, tainted his praise and worship, and infected his spirit of truth with lies. The frightening detail missed by many is pride was founded right in the presences of God. Which says I can be anointed and still accumulate pride right in the presences of God.

The deception of pride is you can have all the signs of success (blessings, possessions, influence) that says you are pleasing to God, only to find that God is displeased by a dreadful fall. We see this with King Saul, as Samson the judge, and so

---

[24] "Helel", http://biblehub.com/hebrew/1966.htm (Accessed March, 24, 2017)

many others of the word of God. Each one somehow overtime mastered the Luciferian Principle that says "*I know how to stand with God in doctrine but defy Him in principle*". I know how to manipulate the strands of love without ever fallen in love. This principle drafts you to become a Luciferian Worshipper, where we see many operating in mantles (gifts and anointings), without ever tapping into the true power of submission and humility. The prophetic ministry is a ministry that must stay in the art of humility for God's usage. Furthermore, the danger of this soul disease (pride) is that it will take you further than you want to go, and keep you longer than you want to stay. The great singer named Hayley Williams stated "sometimes it takes a good fall to really know where you stand". The cure to the spirit of pride is the revelation locked in this oxymoron quoted by the psalmist of Psalms 119:71 (KJV); "it was good for me that I have been afflicted; that I might learn thy statutes". The antidotes injected by God entitled AFFLICTION, HUMILITY, and HUMILIATION.

*Many are the afflictions of the righteous: but the LORD delivereth him out of them all. Psalms 34:19 KJV*

*When pride comes, then comes disgrace, but with humility comes wisdom. Proverbs 11:2 NIV*

# I AM PROPHECY
# PRINCIPLE TWENTY-FIVE:
# DANCING WITH VULTURES
## (PROPHETS AND ANTI-PROPHETS)

> **"EAGLES AND VULTURES ARE BORN FROM THE SAME CREATIVE FAMILY. THE DIFFERENCE IS THE EAGLE EATS RAW AILMENT WHICH IS CAUGHT, WHILE THE VULTURE EATS THE DECAY OF ANOTHER CREATURE'S WORK. THE CONTRASTING IDENTIFICATION BETWEEN PROPHETS AND ANTI-PROPHETS IS REVELATION AND RESIDUE".**

*"Blow the trumpet! Sound the alarm! VULTURES are circling over God's people…" Hosea 8:1a (MSG)*

When understanding the prophetic ministry comprehending symbolism is essential. In prophetic language the prophet is represented by the eagle (Hebrew nesher [25]). The interesting fact of the Accipitridae (the eagle family) is that the vulture (better known as the buzzard) is apart of this species. Represented by the same Hebrew term *nesher* in certain translations; in the bible you find eagle and vulture are interchangeable in scriptures. The eagle is such a majestic image, while the vulture is not as quite romanticizing. Each attribute of both species (the eagle and the vulture) are powerful in imagery. The eagle has a major wingspan, with a white head (the bald eagle), white tail. The vulture is somewhat smaller than the eagle, but has a graceful wingspan just as the eagle. With a bald red head, topped with dark black and brownish tones. Both the eagle and the vulture have superb eyesight but the differentiation of both is major in vastness.

---

[25] "Nesher", http://biblehub.com/hebrew/5404.htm (Accessed March 24,2017)

---

# The Art of Offense

As you see the eagle and the vulture are similar but they are gravely different as well. Just as the Prophet of God and the Anti-Prophet of Satan. As we dive deeper into this divine disclosure just because a vessel is an anti-prophet does not mean they will necessarily have false prophecies. Anti-prophets can have true prophecies but will promote self-exaltation (Is. 47:10) as one of their defining features. However; one of the considerable characteristics of the eagle and the vulture that is found in the vulture. The vulture is an offensive creature, the vulture uses its urine and the urine of its mate to clean itself or to justify its offensive nature. The urine of the vulture kills the bacteria from the decay or carcass it eats. As so does anti-prophets or those of variance, who use others defilement and issues to cover and justify their own problems or issues. The bible calls this action malice, which is a root word that makes up the term malicious. *Malicious is defined as intentionally harm, spiteful behaviors, vicious, wanton, or mischievous in motive or purpose.*[26] *Proverbs 11:9 (KJV) supports this attribute with stating (paraphrasing), hypocrites destroys neighbors with their mouth.* Not only does the vulture uses its urine, it has a defense mechanism of regurgitating (vomiting) on its predator or threat, when threatened or in harm's way. Which also has a prophetic symbol of spewing slander (Pro. 16:28 KJV). As you see the anti-prophet cannot control their mouths, defying the divine principle of studying to be silent (1 Thess. 4:11 KJV). In using others imperfections to perfect themselves.

---

[26] "Malicious". Dictionary.com. *Dictionary.com Unabridged.* Random House, Inc. http://www.dictionary.com/browse/malicious (Accessed Jan. 17, 2017)

# The Lack of Praise

Vultures don't possess a syrinx and nearly are silent while the eagle possess a syrinx. Vultures make a hissing sound, limited to typical vocalizations and grunts, while eagles cry with a resounding pitch. Another faculty of anti-prophetic vessels is the lack of praise, while praise is commonly for the upright (Ps. 33:1 KJV) the true Prophets of God. The inability to exalt God in truth without self-exaltation is nearly impossible for an anti-prophetic vessel. We see this thoroughly in the church of the 21st century; where we have prophetic vessel, believers, even leaders of the church who are gifted but obtain no praise. *Is. 38:18 NLT states "For the grave cannot praise you, death cannot sing your praise; those who go down to the pit cannot hope for your faithfulness".* Those who are dead in spirit cannot praise God or show forth true worship unto God. Those who worship God must worship God in the art of self-truth and in the Spirit of God (John 4:23 KJV). To present self-truth is not the goal of an anti-prophetic vessel, but again self-exaltation which impedes self-exposure.

# Residue or Revelation

Vultures are renownly known for their appetite for carcasses and leftovers (road kill). As eagles are renowned for their graceful ability to hunt from the sea with its majestic features (elegant wings, strong beck, superb eyesight, and powerful talons). The vulture lives off the residue or the remains of another creature's work, while the eagle hunts, seeks, and labour for its possession. The Prophet of God seeks the face of God for fresh revelation from God, while anti-prophets live off of the residue of others hard work. Praying and seeking God according to 2 Chr. 2:17 (KJV) is an core scripture for a true prophetic vessel of God.

# The Absence of Humility

In my studies I found that a vulture circles its prey observing for movement. The power of this technique is that it does not matter if it's prey is living, long as the prey is paralyzed (immovable). While vultures are circling in the air this technique is called a *wake*. This term wake used by the vulture is the same wake humanity use for the viewing of the deceased the day before the funeral. Waiting to see if the prey is really enable to get up or live. No matter what one feels, they have to keep moving in order to denounce the anti-prophecies and words against their purpose. When the clan of vultures land some scientist call this a viewing to examine the prey, because a vulture's strength is not on the ground but in the air. Long as the vulture is flying it has strength but when landed it losses its strength. In prophetic language, low is defined as humbleness or humility. Anti-prophets only can function when they are high or being seen. Jesus denounced this when he spoke of serving. The servant, the one not desiring the high seat but the seat in the lowest parts (Luk. 14:8-10 KJV). Humility is essential in being anointed by God.

# Can You Dance with Vultures?

Eagles and Vultures are both related but one signifies the will of God and the operations of the true prophetic ministry, while the other represents the operations of the carnal man and the demonic realm. The church stands on the true institution of the prophetic ministry, without the prophetic ministry, guidance towards the true perfected will for the church is impractical. The churches objective is not to try to kill or separate vultures but to continue praising and pursuing purpose no matter the circumstances. God will separate the wheat from the tares according to Matt. 13:24-30 (KJV). We must Dance with Vultures in order to see the perfected will of God. Don't be dismayed when you see vultures circling, vultures are a sign something has died. Knowing that to die in Christ is to literally gain in Christ should make you excited and joyful. Even though something has died or is dying, does not mean it cannot be RESURRECTED! Command your prophecy to live, and to keep moving! It's not OVER yet!

*"If my people, which are called by my name, shall humble themselves, and pray, and seek my face, and turn from their wicked ways; then will I hear from heaven, and will forgive their sin, and will heal their land." 2 Chr. 7:14 KJV*

# AFTERWORD

Prophet Orin Perry serves as one of the few authentic Prophets of the millennial generation, who possess the heart of God. He serves dully as one of our Covenant Pastors and Prophets of T.O.P.I.F.C (The Temple of Praise International Fellowship of Churches under Presiding Bishop Glen A. Staples) and H.G.A.A.A (Higher Ground Always Abounding Assemblies). Where I personally serve as the 1st Vice Presiding Prelate of T.O.P.I.F.C and on the board of Bishop's in H.G.A.A.A with Dr. Sherman Watkins (Presiding Prelate), Bishop T.D Jakes (1st Presiding Prelate), and Bishop Glen A. Staples (2nd Presiding Prelate). I was introduced to Prophet Orin Perry's ministry and heart one Holy Convocation where he ministered with such grace, along the likes of Bishop Glen A. Staples, Bishop T.D Jakes, Dr. Cornel West, myself, and so many other great voices in the kingdom of God. Watching him stand in the grace of God reminds me of Timothy the successor of the Apostle Paul who stood with unfeigned faith, wisdom, and boldness without wavering.

Prophet Orin Perry is a dynamic and creative thinker, and is certainly right on in his presentation of "I Am Prophecy." He understands the ways in which the sometime radical and liberating message of prophecy addresses the concerns of the Biblical time line of modern society. "I Am Prophecy" captivates Orin Perry's deep sense of what is going on from a Biblical perceptive and how it relates to life on this planet earth.

**Bishop Fred T. Simms, Th.D.**
**Heart of God Ministries**
**Beckley, West Virginia**

# JOURNALING

# BIBLIOGRAPHY

Cheatham, Dan. The Production of Prophecy. *Five Levels of Prophecy* (2009): http://www.devotional.net/uploads/147/95649.pdf

*Dake Annotated Reference Bible-kjv-large Print*. large ed. Lawrenceville, GA: Dake Publishing, 1999.

Dictionary.com Unabridged. Random House, Inc.

*Encarta World English Dictionary*, [North American Edition], 1998-2003 Microsoft Corporation

Merriam-Webster Online Dictionary copyright © 2015 by Merriam-Webster, Incorporated.

Thomas, Nigel J.T., "Mental Imagery", *The Stanford Encyclopedia of Philosophy* (Spring 2017 Edition), Edward N. Zalta (ed.), URL = <https://plato.stanford.edu/archives/spr2017/entries/mental-imagery/>.

Oxford Dictionaries. Oxford University Press.

Reid, Larry. *The Five-Fold Minister's Reference Book.* (Larry Reid, 2012)

Strong, James. *The Strongest Strong's Exhaustive Concordance of the Bible*. 2-century ed. Grand Rapids, Mich.: Zondervan, 2001.

Wikipedia.org. https://en.wiktionary.org/wiki

# ABOUT THE AUTHOR

Prophet Orin Perry - known as a pastor, intellectual, rare orator, an old man incarcerated in a young body, one whom migrates the mind and voice of God to earth, educator, uncle, brother, and loyal friend serves as the Senior Prophet and Founder of the House of Mandate. Located in Roanoke Rapids, NC, the House of Mandate, under the leadership of Prophet Perry, is one of the cities fastest growing churches. It is a church known for sound prophetic biblical teaching and high praise and worship.

Prophet Perry currently serves as a Covenant Pastor and Prophet under the Temple of Praise International Fellowship of Churches where his pastor is Bishop Glen A. Staples, Th.D. He also serves as a North Carolina District Pastor within the Higher Ground Always Abounding Assemblies, Inc. under the direction of Bishop Dr. Sherman S. Watkins, Prelate; Bishop T. D. Jakes, Vice-Prelate; and Bishop Dr. Glen A. Staples, 2nd Vice-Prelate. Prophet Perry has been graced to minister up to 14,000 people and minister on platforms with some of the most renowned voices of the church. Such as Bishop T.D Jakes, Pastor Sheryl Brady, Dr. Jamal Bryant, Bishop George G. Bloomer, and Dr. Marvin Sapp just to name a few.

Prophet Perry was called to the gospel ministry at the tender age of six. He served as a spiritual son in the Way of the Cross Church for seventeen years under the tutelage of the late Dr. Martha S. Parker of The Way of the Cross. In 2008, God led him to his current spiritual father Bishop Dr. Glen A. Staples of the Temple of Praise, Washington, D.C, where he currently serves in sonship. In 2011, Prophet Perry founded The House of Mandate (HOM) in an effort to address church hurts, spiritual obscurity, personal insecurity, and give biblical truths that people can apply to everyday circumstances. Prophet preaches the WORD, which transcends all genders, denominations, distresses, immoral acts, and voices "Jesus died a pugnacious death, so you can live a prosperous life."

Under the leadership of Prophet Orin Perry, The House of Mandate, in addition to sound biblical teaching, prophetic training, and leadership workshops, offers the community classes on resume building, financial management, and business entrepreneurship. Through a partnership with a local community college, the church will soon offer GED, continuing education, and business management courses.

Born in Roanoke Rapids, NC, Pastor Perry attended Halifax County schools. He holds an Associates and a Bachelor's of Science in Psychology. His wisdom and keen insight continues to be featured and sought out. He is the author of *"I AM PROPHECY"*, a daily prophetic study for *"Prophetic Preliminaries"*.

Prophet Perry has been featured on several national televised networks - TBN (Trinity Broadcast Network), The Word Network, TCTtv (Tri-State Christian Television), The Impact Network, TCN (The Comcast Network), and radio 107.3 WBOB-FM (The Promise - Rocky Mount, NC). Recently, Prophet Perry joined Halifax County School District in launching a young men's empowerment program to prepare the Adams of today to take their position as not only the head, but also the mind and brains in society.

Serving dually as a prophet and pastor, Prophet Perry's mission is to mold his congregation, and anyone who can benefit therefrom, into powerful intercessors in the church, community, the world, or even the universe. Don't be fooled by the container that you see, but be wise enough to drink from the content in the container in him that you don't see.

# CONTACT INFORMATION

**Orin Perry Ministries Inc.**
www.orinperry.com
(252) 518-1918

**Mailing:**
P.O Box 517
Roanoke Rapids N.C. 27870

**Physical Address:**
1510 B Buffaloe St
Roanoke Rapids N.C. 27870